Exploratory Spanish For Middle School

Written By:
Tom Alsop
Jill Alsop

Managing Editor:
Ryan R. West

Page Layout Artist:
Rebecca Cober

ISBN: 978-0-7560-0145-2
SKU: B5
Printed in Roseville, MI •1206GRA

OVERVIEW

Activities in this book include vocabulary, conversation, and culture. The book focuses on the national standards of comparisons, communication, and culture. Structure is deliberately kept simple [mostly present tense], with the basic elements necessary for meaningful conversations.

HOW TO

1. Make copies of the three-page topic you want your students to study.
2. Hand out the pages to the class. Model the *Vocabulario* section aloud with the class.
3. Have students work in pairs or groups of three or four, following the instructions to complete the other activities covered in each topic.
4. Collect the papers and assign grades for the students' work.
5. Have students keep a vocabulary notebook listing and writing sentences with each new word learned.
6. Assign Enrichment Section as homework.

TIME

Each project will take 35-40 minutes to complete.

INDEX

Parte Uno-Lengua
Temas-capítulos

Parte Dos-Cultura

Parte Uno-Lengua

El alfabeto
Los saludos
Los números
La hora del día
La ropa
Los colores
El tiempo
Los objetos de clase
El verbo gustar
Las palabras interrogativas
La familia
El cuerpo
Los cuartos de la casa
Los días/los meses
El verbo ser
El verbo estar
El verbo tener
El verbo ir
La comida
Los sustantivos/adjetivos

www.teachersdiscovery.com

1-El alfabeto

Name: _____

Date: _____

Class: _____

Vocabulario

Read and say the following words out loud and in Spanish with your teacher.

a-a	**k**-ka	**s**-ese
b-be	**l**-ele	**t**-te
c-ce	**m**-eme	**u**-u
d-de	**n**-ene	**v**-ve
e-e	**ñ** eñe	**w**-doble ve
f-efe	**o**-o	**x**-equis
g-ge	**p**-pe	**y**-i griega
h-hache	**q**-cu	**z**-zeta
i-i	**r**-ere	
j-jota		

Crucigrama

Work with a classmate to complete the following crossword puzzle.

Across

1. i
2. r
3. v
4. z
6. ñ
9. l

Down

1. y
5. n
7. m
8. t

1-El alfabeto

Conversación

With a classmate, read and say the following dialogue between two classmates at a school in Arizona.

Carmen:	Hola, Alfonso.
Alfonso:	Buenos días, Carmen.
Carmen:	¡Vamos a practicar (*Let's practice*) el alfabeto!
Alfonso:	Buena idea.(*Good idea*)
Carmen:	¿Cómo se escribe la palabra(*How do you write the word*)"hola"?
Alfonso:	Hache,o,ele,a.
Carmen:	¡Fabuloso, Alfonso!
Alfonso:	¿Cómo se escribe la palabra, "adiós"?
Carmen:	A,de,i,o,ese.
Alfonso:	Perfecto, Carmen. Hasta luego.
Carmen:	Hasta mañana.

Teatro

You are having a spelling bee in your Spanish class. Work in groups of three. One person is the teacher and will give the words. The other two are students and will spell the words in Spanish. Include vocabulary from the **Vocabulario** and **Conversación** sections. Include at least four sentences for each person.

_____

_____

_____

_____

_____

_____

_____

With a classmate pretend you are an airline reservationist taking information over the phone from a customer. Ask the customer how to spell his/her first *(nombre)* and last name *(apellido)*. Also ask him/her how to spell his street name *(la calle)*. Include vocabulary from the **Vocabulario** and **Conversación** sections.

_____

_____

_____

_____

A
ALSOP

2

1-El alfabeto

Name: _____

Date: _____

Class: _____

Juego
With a classmate, write the word these letters are spelling. Do you know the English meaning?

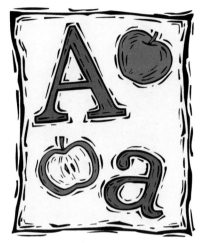

1. e,ese,pe,a,eñe,o,ele _____
2. ce,ele,a,ese,e _____
3. eme,a,pe,a _____
4. eme,u,ese,i,ce,a _____
5. be,a,ene,de,a _____
6. a,i,ere,e _____
7. ese,e,eñe,o,ere _____
8. efe,a,ve,o,ere,i,te,o _____
9. zeta,o,ene,a _____
10. ce,ele,a,ese,i,ce,o _____

Proyecto
In groups of four, make a Spanish picture dictionary. Each person will be responsible for seven letters of the alphabet. Find a word that begins with the letters you have in a Spanish dictionary. Then draw a picture for each word. Be neat and use color. When complete, share your dictionary with the rest of the class.

Enrichment - internet
With a classmate, find a Web site that gives Spanish vocabulary for animals. List the Web site address and six words you found. Then spell them out using the Spanish alphabet.

_____
_____
_____
_____
_____
_____

www.teachersdiscovery.com

ALSOP

2-Los saludos

Name: _____

Date: _____

Class: _____

Vocabulario
Read and say the following words out loud and in Spanish with your teacher.

Buenos días-good morning
Buenas noches-good night
Adiós-goodbye
¿Cómo se llama usted?-What's your name?
Me llamo................. -My name is ....
¿Cómo está usted?-How are you?
Estoy bien.-I am fine.
Estoy muy bien.-I am very fine.
Estoy así, así.-I am so-so.
Gracias-Thanks
Por favor-Please
Mucho gusto-Nice meeting you
El gusto es mío.-The pleasure is mine.

Buenas tardes-good afternoon
Hola-hello
Hasta luego-see you later

Crucigrama
With a classmate, complete the following crossword puzzle.

Across
3. my name is
6. fine
8. good night
9. *buenas* afternoon
10. hello

Down
1. please
2. goodbye
4. good morning
5. thanks
7. nice meeting you

2-Los saludos

Name: _____

Date: _____

Class: _____

Conversación

With a classmate, read and say the following dialogue between two teenagers at a school in Colorado.

Marta:	Hola, buenos días. ¿Cómo te llamas?
Carlos:	Me llamo Carlos. ¿Y tú, cómo te llamas?
Marta:	Me llamo Marta. ¿Cómo estás?
Carlos:	Bien, gracias. ¿Y tú?
Marta:	Muy bien, gracias.
Carlos:	Pues, mucho gusto.
Marta:	El gusto es mío.
Carlos:	Adiós.
Marta:	Adiós. Hasta luego.

Teatro

With a classmate, role play that you are students meeting for the first time at your school. Introduce yourselves. Write a six-sentence conversation that takes place between the two of you. Include vocabulary from the **Vocabulario** and **Conversación** sections.

_____
_____
_____
_____
_____
_____

With a classmate, role play that you are meeting a Latin American student at your school. Introduce yourselves. Use appropriate greetings. Write a six-sentence conversation that takes place between the two of you. Include vocabulary from the **Vocabulario** and **Conversación** sections.

_____
_____
_____
_____
_____
_____
_____

A
ALSOP

5

2-Los saludos

Name: _____

Date: _____

Class: _____

Juego
With a classmate, unscramble these Spanish words and then give the meaning in English.

1. laho
2- sída uebsno
3- sadió
4. tahsa uelog
5. satred uebnsa
6. cehons eunbsa
7. nibe
8. saí, sía
9. rofav rop
10. crgaisa

_____
_____
_____
_____
_____
_____
_____
_____
_____
_____

Proyecto
Work in pairs. Do a greeting card in Spanish using some basic *saludos*. Include appropriate vocabulary and some drawings. Practice in the space below. Do the greeting card on another paper. Color the drawings!

Enrichment - Dibujemos
With a classmate, draw a first time encounter between a new student at school and one of your friends. Label the appropriate greetings in Spanish.

3-Los números

Name: _____

Date: _____

Class: _____

Vocabulario
Read and say the following words out loud and in Spanish with your teacher.

1-uno	11-once
2-dos	12-doce
3-tres	13-trece
4-cuatro	14-catorce
5-cinco	15-quince
6-seis	16-dieciséis
7-siete	17-diecisiete
8-ocho	18-dieciocho
9-nueve	19-diecinueve
10-diez	20-veinte

Crucigrama
With a classmate, complete the following word search.

```
M E X J E D I E C I O C H O Q S G L S H      CATORCE
O Q C V K D D A T O F T X U W E V I N A      CINCO
O P E N S F X E J E G Z I N S I É C G B      CUATRO
G U B D O Y E T V K I N S K X S D U R H      DIECINUEVE
N H P V V D C O R G C S D J I C R A X F      DIECIOCHO
E T N I E V N A L E B P I C X S S T O S      DIECISIETE
K R Z Y C V K T R K S L E C T R X R U F      DIECISÉIS
B N Q U O B P L P H C I X T E Q Z O P T      DIEZ
C M C Q D R V C Q A D C T V I I R L P U      DOCE
H A Z E I D Y E Y E L Q D O S C D P T Y      DOS
M W T Z O B F B C G H Z H H Q W D K E N      NUEVE
R K P O C W O J K Q J R G E Z P P G V T      OCHO
L S D V R C J O Y M F X M H T T W S E D      ONCE
X Q W O H C Q Z E M N J D G H V M I U E      QUINCE
G Z N O I Y E Y H M S K C V O D C J N T      SEIS
O U O S A B L J J I U Z S Q D L A D I E      SIETE
S C U F Z X E H M P R D U F Q H Q G C I      TRECE
Z E N N E Y K W H B O V E L W Y Y A E S      TRES
R H G I M H S G A J O T S B K U X S I E      UNO
N T R E C E U V K C Q F X V R G O B D V      VEINTE
```

3-Los números

Name: _____

Date: _____

Class: _____

Conversación
With a classmate, read and say the following dialogue between a math teacher and one of her/his students.

Emilio:	Hola, buenos días, señorita Arias.
Srta. Arias:	Hola, Emilio. ¿Cómo estás?
Emilio:	Muy bien, gracias. Señorita, ¡yo sé(*I know*)los números en español!
Srta. Arias:	¡Fantástico! Por favor, cuente hasta(*up to*)diez.
Emilio:	Uno, dos, tres, cuatro, cinco, seis, siete, ocho, nueve, diez.
Srta. Arias:	¡Fabuloso! Tú eres(*You are*)un Albert Einstein.
Emilio:	Gracias. Y ahora al revés: diez, nueve, ocho, siete, seis, cinco, cuatro, tres, dos, uno.
Srta. Arias:	¡Tú eres un estudiante superior!
Emilio:	Gracias, señorita Arias. Me gustan(*I like*)los números.

Teatro
With a classmate, role play that you are studying the Spanish numbers with a classmate. Write a six-sentence conversation that takes place between the two of you. Include vocabulary from the **Vocabulario** and **Conversación** sections.

_____
_____
_____
_____
_____
_____

With a classmate, pretend that you meet a new student at your school. Introduce yourselves. Ask how he/she is feeling. Ask where he/she is from and exchange telephone numbers(*número telefónico*) with each other Write a six-sentence conversation that takes place between the two of you. Include vocabulary from the **Vocabulario** and **Conversación**

_____
_____
_____
_____

A
ALSOP

8

3-Los números

Name: _____

Date: _____

Class: _____

Juego

Working with a classmate, can you solve these Spanish math problems? Write the answer in Spanish.

1. dos+cinco= _____
2. tres+diez= _____
3. cuatro+cinco= _____
4. ocho+once= _____
5. quince+cinco= _____
6. dieciocho-siete= _____
7. dieciséis-ocho= _____
8. doce-ocho= _____
9. tres-dos= _____
10. siete-uno= _____

Proyecto

Working with a classmate, create your own dot-to-dot picture. Instead of using numerals, write the Spanish numbers in words. Use a minimum of 12 numbers, but try for up to *veinte*! Have the teacher make copies. Then connect the dots and color! Try some your classmates have made!

Enrichment - Dibujemos

With a classmate, design and draw five new license plates for use next year. Use letters and numbers on the license plates. Write the numbers as words. Be sure to make them colorful! When you are done, practice saying them in Spanish to your partner!

A
ALSOP

9

4-La hora del dia

Name: _____

Date: _____

Class: _____

Vocabulario
Read and say the following words out loud and in Spanish with your teacher.

¿Qué hora es?- What time is it?
Es la una.- It is 1:00 o'clock.
Son las dos-doce. - It is 2-12 o'clock.
Son las tres y cinco. - It is 3:05
Son las cinco y cuarto. - It is 5:15.
Son las seis y media. - It is 6:30.
Son las ocho menos diez. - It is 7:50.
Son las once menos veinte. - It is 10:40.

Es mediodía.- It is noon.
Es medianoche.- It is midnight.

de la mañana - A.M.
de la tarde - P.M. (1-7)
de la noche - P.M. (8-12)
¿A qué hora? - at what time

Across
6. It is 5:10.

Down
1. a.m.
2. It is 7:50.
3. It is 1:00.
4. p.m.
5. It is midnight.

Crucigrama
Complete the following crossword puzzle.

4-La hora del dia

Name: _____

Date: _____

Class: _____

Conversación

With a classmate, read and say the following dialogue between two teenagers at a school in California.

Rosa:	Hola Memo, ¿cómo estás?
Memo:	Fantástico, Rosa. ¿Y tú?
Rosa:	Bien, gracias. ¿Qué hora es, Memo?
Memo:	Son las dos y veinticinco.
Rosa:	Mi clase de inglés es a las dos y media.
Memo:	Rosa, el concierto de Enrique Iglesias es a las ocho de la noche.
Rosa:	Sí, Memo. Te veo (*I'll see you*) a las siete y media, ¿verdad? (*right?*)
Memo:	Sí, hasta luego.
Rosa:	Adiós. Hasta pronto.

Teatro

With a classmate, role play that you are friends having a conversation at school. Greet each other and ask how you are feeling. Write a six-sentence conversation that takes place between the two of you. Ask what time it is and confirm the time for an evening activity. Include vocabulary from the **Vocabulario** and **Conversación** sections.

_____
_____
_____
_____
_____
_____

With a classmate, role play that one of you is an exchange student at your school. Introduce yourselves. Use appropriate greetings. Write a six-sentence conversation about what time it is and at what time various classes begin. Include vocabulary from the **Vocabulario** and **Conversación** sections.

_____
_____
_____
_____
_____

A

ALSOP

11

4-La hora del dia

Name: _____

Date: _____

Class: _____

Juego
With a classmate, unscramble these Spanish words and then give the meaning in English.

1. roah   _____
2. deima   _____
3. enco   _____
4. rcouta   _____
5. amhendcioe _____
6. adetr   _____
7. mosen   _____
8. anamña   _____
9. uéq   _____
10. nua   _____

Proyecto
Work in pairs. Use paper plates to make a clock face. Draw the hands on the clock. On the back of the plate, write the time in English and Spanish. Use color and remember to make the numbers large enough so the whole class can see! Take turns using the paper clocks to practice saying the time in Spanish with your partners. Exchange your clocks with other groups for more practice.

Enrichment - Dibujemos
With a classmate, draw five funny clocks with different times. Write the time below the clock in Spanish.

5-La ropa

Vocabulario
Read and say the following words out loud and in Spanish with your teacher.

el sombrero - hat	**los calcetines** - socks
la gorra - cap	**los zapatos de tenis** - tennis shoes
la camisa - shirt	**el cinturón** - belt
los pantalones - slacks	**la sudadera** - sweat shirt
el vestido - dress	**la camiseta** - T-shirt
la falda - skirt	**la ropa interior** - underwear
los zapatos - shoes	**los guantes** - gloves
la chaqueta - jacket	**la bufanda** - scarf
el abrigo - coat	**el pañuelo** - handkerchief
el suéter - sweater	**la corbata** - tie
el traje - men's suit	**los vaqueros** - blue jeans
la blusa - blouse	

Sopa de Letras
Find and circle the Spanish words listed below.

```
L F O V P F Q T P L D L J K J V L T L W
O O A D A G Q A A R O V O Q X V O Y A F
S T S Q K A Z B A S I M A C A L G V C Z
C A L P F H U D V R M Z S A M A S F O O
A R T B A F F A Q A Q B A D V V B F R Z
L U I E A N Q I T P G R H W G L U H B Q
C U O N U U T E R Q L U M V N I C A A A
E M D O E Q S A O R E R B M O S L E T C
T A E R Q I A J L D W A G J R V N Y A E
I F O L M E R H B O P G J N U O M F P B
N S E A V A V L C W N O L F T Y M Q W T
E A C G U E V K O A S E M A N D U J Q E
S A B W S J S Y U G L C S Q I Z Q F J T
L O S G U A N T E S I I N Z C G T A A A
M L A B L U S A I G R R R L L R R M E R
M G B O Z X U T W D K I B G E T A F H R
H K U O Y H S F U O O Q P A L P N W R O
H W S O J V X K E P Z J A E L C L B W G
A U C S T X X E E S T D A A D E W E V A
L G O L O G U J E S V A X L Y A C J V L
```

EL ABRIGO
EL CINTURÓN
EL SOMBRERO
EL TRAJE
EL VESTIDO
LA BLUSA
LA BUFANDA
LA CAMISA
LA CAMISETA
LA CHAQUETA
LA CORBATA
LA GORRA
LOS CALCETINES
LOS GUANTES
LOS PANTALONES
LOS VAQUEROS

5-La ropa

Conversación

With a classmate, read and say the following dialogue between two friends at a school in New Jersey.

Bertha:	Hola, Javier. ¡Qué guapo! (*How handsome!*) ¡Me gusta tu ropa! (*I like your clothes!*)
Javier:	Pues, gracias, Bertha. Mis vaqueros son nuevos(*new*). La sudadera es de España.
Bertha:	¿Y los zapatos de tenis?
Javier:	Los compré anoche en la zapatería (*I bought them last night at the shoe store.*) Y tu falda es muy bonita. ¿Dónde la compraste (*Where did you buy it*)?
Bertha:	La compré (*I bought it*) en la tienda de ropa (*at the clothing store*) cerca de aquí (*near here*).
Javier:	Pues, me gusta ir de compras. (*I like to go shopping.*)
Bertha:	A mí también. (*Me too.*)
Javier:	Pues, que pases un buen día. (*Well, have a nice day.*)
Bertha:	Gracias, que te vaya bien. (*Thanks, may you have a nice day.*)

Teatro

With a classmate, role play that you are friends discussing your new clothes. Say in Spanish what new clothes you have. Include vocabulary from the **Vocabulario** and **Conversación** sections. Use *tengo* (I have) whenever possible. Write the dialogue and then say out loud. Include three sentences for each person.

_____

_____

_____

_____

_____

_____

With a classmate, role play that you are telling a store clerk what clothes you like. Use *me gusta* (I like) whenever possible. Write a six-sentence conversation that takes place between the two of you. Include vocabulary from the **Vocabulario** and **Conversación** sections.

_____

_____

_____

_____

_____

A

ALSOP

14

5-La ropa

Name: _____

Date: _____

Class: _____

Juego
With a classmate, unscramble these Spanish words and then give the meaning in English.

1. ldfaa _____
2. suganet _____
3. tocrbaa _____
4. stvedio _____
5. cmasia _____
6. pozaast _____
7. ntpalanose _____
8. bsormreo _____
9. dasuedar _____
10. ublas _____

Proyecto
Work in pairs. Plan a fashion show. One student will model the clothes and the other will say what the model is wearing. Use "*lleva*"(wears, is wearing) in the description. Example: *María lleva una blusa y una falda. También lleva unos zapatos bonitos.*

Enrichment - Dibujemos
Draw a picture of five of your favorite articles of clothing. Label them in Spanish.

6 - Los colores

Name: _____

Date: _____

Class: _____

Vocabulario
Read and say the following words out loud and in Spanish with your teacher.

blanco -white
rojo - red
verde - green
amarillo - yellow
rosado - pink
marrón - brown

negro - black
azul - blue
gris - gray
anaranjado - orange
violeta - purple
turquesa - turquoise

Crucigrama
With a classmate, complete the following crossword puzzle.

Across
1. turquoise
4. gray
8. orange
9. purple
11. black

Down
2. yellow
3. brown
5. pink
6. white
7. green
10. blue

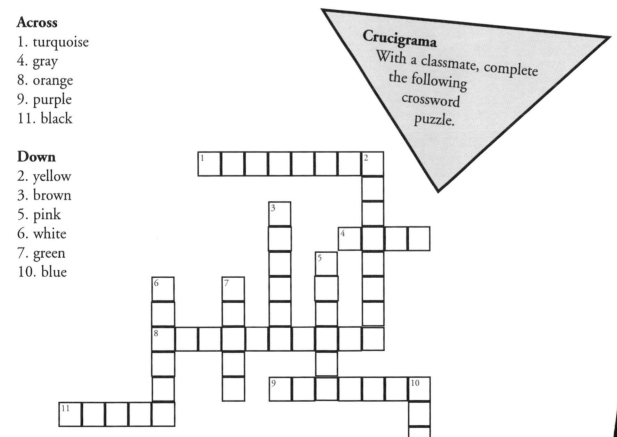

www.teachersdiscovery.com

ALSOP

6 - Los colores

Name: _____

Date: _____

Class: _____

Conversación
With a classmate, read and say the following dialogue between two art students at a middle school in Florida.

Rafa:	Hola, Tina. ¿Cómo estás?
Tina:	Así, así, Rafa. ¿Y tú?
Rafa:	Bien, gracias. ¿Cuál es (*What is*) tu color favorito, Tina?
Tina:	Me gustan (*I like*) los colores rojo y violeta.
Rafa:	Me gustan los colores azul y negro.
Tina:	También (*also*) me gusta el color amarillo.
Rafa:	Tengo prisa (*I'm in a hurry*). Adiós, Tina.
Tina:	Hasta la vista, Rafa.

Teatro
With a classmate, role play that the two of you are in art class and are talking about your favorite colors. Write a six-sentence conversation that takes place between the two of you. Include vocabulary from the **Vocabulario** and **Conversación** sections.

_____
_____
_____
_____
_____
_____

With a classmate, role play that you meet Pablo Picasso at an art museum. Introduce yourself. Use appropriate greetings. Write a six-sentence conversation that takes place between the two of you. Include vocabulary from the **Vocabulario** and **Conversación** sections.

_____
_____
_____
_____
_____

A
ALSOP

17

6 - Los colores

Juego
With a classmate, unscramble the following Spanish words and then give the meaning in English.

1. rooj   _____
2. renog   _____
3. erdev   _____
4. nadaraanjo _____
5. lonabc   _____
6. rnóamr   _____
7. radoso   _____
8. lauz   _____
9. rsgi   _____
10. milolara _____

Proyecto
Work in pairs. Design a poster to teach the class the colors in Spanish. Include at least eight colors. Be sure to draw pictures to make it more entertaining! Add new colors if you wish.

Enrichment - Dibujemos
Draw and color pictures of something that you associate with six of the colors above. Write the color in Spanish below the picture. See if your classmates can guess what you have drawn.

7 - El tiempo

Vocabulario
Read and say the following words out loud and in Spanish with your teacher.

¿Qué tiempo hace?	What's the weather like?
Hace buen tiempo.	It's good weather.
Hace mal tiempo.	It's bad weather.
Hace sol.	It's sunny.
Hace calor.	It's warm.
Hace viento.	It's windy.
Hace frío.	It's cold.
Hace fresco.	It's cool.
Está lloviendo.	It's raining.
Está nevando.	It's snowing.
Está nublado.	It's cloudy.

Sopa de Letras
Find and circle the following Spanish words.

```
C V F S A X Y D H K X N U D S L O J U U
E G U F X Z W A A H H U G Q T D H N X G
L C W V V V C U C D X A Q J A A U S J C
L O A T T E J I E C U C C L C X H W J R
K O J H F S K D B C K R B E O L Y V Y P
K A C R O S Y C U H N U M H F I G V A B
R C Í W R P L I E G N A U A P R Q W H E
V O W X X C M P N Á L S I C O Q E M C N
I V Y N T M P E T T A F J E D A Q S E L
I L R N R R H S I X D S H C N T Z D C D
Z I K X J R E E E T J H T A A D H T U O
Q B Z T I R M I M K É M W L V W Q N C N
T C U K N P V S P M D U Y O E T K O I U
T D V A O K J P O H D D Q R N V L R B W
H A C E V I E N T O S N R F Á R Q J I H
L O S E C A H I C W N G N M T M C Y H Z
O D N E I V O L L Á T S E F S E J T D Y
T U U Z O U U F I D U F T Z E I V L J W
H F B B F I F E G H N A Q O N U G X D N
V N O I F A J M J Y S B G Z D F K T N K
```

ESTÁ LLOVIENDO
ESTÁ NEVANDO
ESTÁ NUBLADO
HACE BUEN TIEMPO
HACE CALOR
HACE FRESCO
HACE FRÍO
HACE MAL TIEMPO
HACE SOL
HACE VIENTO
¿QUÉ TIEMPO HACE?

A
ALSOP

19

7 - El tiempo

Name: _____

Date: _____

Class: _____

Conversación

With a classmate, read and say the following dialogue between two snow skiers.

Raquel:	Buenos días, Felipe.
Felipe:	Hola, Raquel. ¿Cómo estás?
Raquel:	Bien, gracias. Felipe, ¿quieres esquiar hoy? (*Do you want to ski today?*)
Felipe:	¡Buena idea! (*Good idea!*) ¿Qué tiempo hace?
Raquel:	Hace frío y hace viento.
Felipe:	¿Está nevando?
Raquel:	Sí, un poco (*a little*). Es perfecto, ¿no?
Felipe:	Sí, vámonos (*let's go*)!
Raquel:	Te veo (*I'll see you*) en cinco minutos.
Felipe:	Bueno. Hasta pronto.

Teatro

With a classmate, pretend that you are making plans to go swimming (*nadar*). Discuss the weather first and then decide if you will go. Write a six-sentence conversation that takes place between the two of you. Include vocabulary from the **Vocabulario** and **Conversación**

_____

_____

_____

_____

_____

_____

With a classmate, imagine you are a meteorologist and are working with a colleague to plan the 6:00 weather report. Write a six-sentence conversation that takes place between the two of you. Include vocabulary from the **Vocabulario** and **Conversación** sections.

_____

_____

_____

_____

_____

A
ALSOP

7 - El tiempo

Name: _____

Date: _____

Class: _____

Juego
With a classmate, write in the missing letters and give the English meaning.

THE WEATHER

1. v_en_o   _____
2. _res_o   _____
3. so_   _____
4. n_van_o   _____
5. ca_o_   _____
6. ti_m_o   _____
7. nub_ad_   _____
8. m_l   _____
9. l_o_iendo   _____
10. _ace   _____

Proyecto
In groups of three, prepare a weather forecast for television. Make a poster showing the place, the weather in picture form, and the necessary Spanish phrases. Give your weather forecast to the class. You may even want to videotape it!

Enrichment - internet
With a classmate, find a Web site that gives the weather. Record the weather in Madrid (Spain), Santiago (Chile), San Juan (Puerto Rico), and Mexico City (Mexico). Write in Spanish, of course!

_____
_____
_____
_____
_____
_____
_____

A

ALSOP

21

8 - Los objetos de clase

Name: _____

Date: _____

Class: _____

Vocabulario

Read and say the following words out loud and in Spanish with your teacher.

el lápiz - pencil
el papel - paper
el cuaderno - notebook
el diccionario - dictionary
la mochila - backpack

el bolígrafo - pen
la carpeta - folder
el libro - book
la regla - ruler
la calculadora - calculator

Crucigrama
With a classmate, complete the following crossword puzzle.

Across
4. folder
6. paper
7. pencil
8. dictionary
9. notebook

Down
1. book
2. backpack
3. ruler
4. calculator
5. pen

8 - Los objetos de clase

Name: _____

Date: _____

Class: _____

Conversación

With a classmate, read and say the following dialogue between two students in the school

Elena:	Hola Nacho, ¿cómo estás?
Nacho:	Fantástico, Elena. ¿Y tú?
Elena:	Bien, gracias. Necesito algunas cosas (*I need some things*) para mis clases.
Nacho:	¿Qué necesitas? (*What do you need?*)
Elena:	Necesito dos lápices, un paquete de papel y una regla.
Nacho:	Aquí están (*here they are*), Elena. ¿Algo más? (*Anything else?*)
Elena:	Sí, Nacho, dos carpetas y un bolígrafo.
Nacho:	Bueno, ¿es todo? (*Is that all?*)
Elena:	Sí, gracias, Nacho.
Nacho:	De nada (*You're welcome*), Elena. Hasta luego.

Teatro

With a classmate, role play that you are friends having a conversation in the school bookstore. Greet each other and ask how you are feeling. Write a six-sentence conversation that takes place between the two of you. Discuss what supplies you need for your school classes. Include vocabulary from the **Vocabulario** and **Conversación** sections.

_____

_____

_____

_____

_____

_____

You are showing your parents your school supply list. Tell them the items you will need for your classes. Include vocabulary from the **Vocabulario** and **Conversación** sections.

_____

_____

_____

_____

ALSOP

23

8 - Los objetos de clase

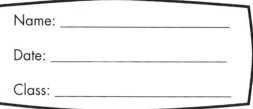

Name: _____

Date: _____

Class: _____

Juego
With a classmate, write the word these letters are spelling. Do you know the English meaning?

1. zápli   _____
2. arelg   _____
3. naucdroe   _____
4. holacim   _____
5. cepatar   _____
6. borli   _____
7. laclarudaco   _____
8. rancoidicio   _____
9. lapep   _____
10. fogarlobí   _____

Proyecto
With a classmate, design an advertisement for a local discount store. The ad is promoting a sale (*venta*) of school supplies for the beginning of the school year. Include four or five supplies, prices, name of store, and sale dates. Include a catchy phrase! Use color. Use as much Spanish as possible in your ad. Take a class vote to see which one is the most creative!

Enrichment - Dibujemos
Draw eight of the classroom supplies. Use color and label each item in Spanish.

9 -El verbo gustar

Name: _____

Date: _____

Class: _____

Vocabulario
Read and say the following words out loud and in Spanish with your teacher.

Me gusta or **me gustan**-I like
Te gusta or **te gustan**-you like
¿Qué clase te gusta?-What class do you like?
la ciencia - science
las matemáticas - math
el inglés - English
el arte - art
la música - music
las ciencias sociales - social studies
la educación física - physical education
el español - Spanish
la computación-computer class

Sopa de Letras

With a classmate, find and circle the following Spanish words.

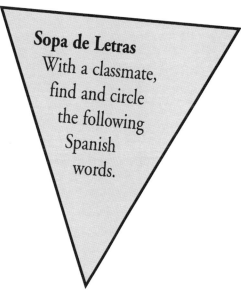

```
E Y O K F P W X Q N V B G W H N Q P O M
T M I N A F W S I Y C A Q R H O D A R E
R F E S W U N L F S L N P L R E S Z R G
A H T G E H B U K E Z B V L U E F W T U
L N E X U C J I P S A X C T S I Z C R S
E K L S T S R M B A M H E A I U B Q H T
A A C R F U T N I L Q G L R S L Q S Q A
T S V M S W L A L C U C J I Y U I V M L
S C U P D Q B L L S S W Q J L E C B O A
U R L M E G U S T A E L E S P A Ñ O L M
G S S C W W C A L L C J Q W R J S T X Ú
E H R X R U L N X N G I U E W K I W P S
T L P W Z A A J R A P J E R Q C V W T I
D X A E C T I A X T G D V N F M G F A C
D H K L S R U S D S R L X I C B Q O Y A
V X A U J Z S N W U V I J P Y I F G N N
N S G I Q S T Q V G U S J C Y V A U W W
E E Q V E T R A L E A T S U G E M R B O
T S A Z Z B P U J M W N Z X E F Q F O Z
Q M I L H M M T F H J I I B F P D W G J
```

ME GUSTA EL ARTE
ME GUSTA EL ESPAÑOL
ME GUSTA LA CIENCIA
ME GUSTA LA MÚSICA
ME GUSTAN LAS CLASES
TE GUSTA EL ARTE
TE GUSTA LA CLASE
TE GUSTAN LAS CLASES

ALSOP
25

9 - El verbo gustar

Conversación

With a classmate, read and say the following dialogue between two friends discussing their likes and dislikes.

Sofía:	Buenas tardes, Ramón.
Ramón:	Hola, Sofía. ¿Qué tal (How's everything) ?
Sofía:	Muy bien, Ramón. Gracias.
Ramón:	Dime (Tell me), Sofía, ¿qué clase te gusta?
Sofía:	Me gusta la clase de arte. ¿Y tú?
Ramón:	Me gusta la clase de música.
Sofía:	¿Te gustan las matemáticas?
Ramón:	No, pero (but) me gustan las ciencias sociales.
Sofía:	Hasta mañana, Ramón.
Ramón:	Adiós, Sofía.

Teatro

Interviewing two classmates for your school newspaper. Ask them what classes they like and what they dislike. Write a six-sentence conversation that takes place between the three of you. Include vocabulary from the **Vocabulario** and **Conversación** sections.

_____

_____

_____

_____

_____

_____

With a classmate, role play that one of you is a new student from Arizona. Discuss the classes you like and dislike. Write a six-sentence conversation that takes place between the two of you. Include vocabulary from the **Vocabulario** and **Conversación** sections.

_____

_____

_____

_____

_____

A

ALSOP

9 - El verbo gustar

Name: _____

Date: _____

Class: _____

Juego

With a classmate, write in the missing letters and give the English meaning.

1 i_glés _____

2. _ienc_a _____

3. g_s_an _____

4. mú_ic_ _____

5. c_a_e _____

6. _spañ_l _____

7. a_ _e _____

8. co_pu_ación _____

9. mat_má_icas _____

10. _ué _____

Proyecto

Take a class survey of what classes your friends like. Then make a bar graph to show the results. Label in Spanish.

Enrichment - internet

With a classmate, find a Web site that gives the names of sports in Spanish. Write Spanish sentences stating which sports you like and dislike.

_____

_____

_____

_____

_____

_____

A

ALSOP

27

10 - Las palabras interrogativas

Vocabulario
Read and say the following words out loud and in Spanish with your teacher.

¿quién? - who
¿qué? - what
¿cuándo? - when
¿dónde? - where
¿cómo? - how
¿por qué? - why

¿Quién?

Proyecto
With a classmate, write a newspaper story about a recent event in your school. Make sure to answer all of the *interrogativas* - who, what, when, where, how, and why!

_____
_____
_____
_____
_____
_____
_____

10 - Las palabras interrogativas

Name: _____

Date: _____

Class: _____

Conversación
With a classmate, read and say the following dialogue between two friends who are talking in a local restaurant.

Paco :	Hola, María. ¿Quién es ese (*that*) chico?
María :	Es Jorge Gómez.
Paco :	¿De dónde es Jorge?
María :	Es de España.
Paco :	¿Qué ciudad (*city*)?
María :	Es de Madrid, la captial.
Paco :	¿Cuándo llegó (*did he arrive*) a los Estados Unidos?
María :	Ayer (*yesterday*).
Paco :	¿Cómo llegó (*did he arrive*)?
María :	En avión (*by plane*).
Paco :	¿Por qué está en los Estados Unidos?
María :	Es un alumno de intercambio (*exchange student*).
Paco :	Gracias, María. Vamos a pedir (*let's order*).

¿Dónde?

Teatro
With a classmate, role play a conversation between a student and his/her mother. You ask her some questions about her friend. Include vocabulary from the **Vocabulario** and **Conversación** sections. Write the dialogue and then say aloud. Include three sentences for each person.

_____
_____
_____
_____
_____
_____

Work in pairs. You are in Spanish class. You ask your teacher some questions. Write a six-sentence conversation that takes place between the two of you. Include vocabulary from the **Vocabulario** and **Conversación** sections.

_____
_____
_____
_____
_____
_____

A
ALSOP

29

10 - Las palabras interrogativas

Name: _____

Date: _____

Class: _____

Juego
With a classmate, unscramble these Spanish words
and then give the meaning in English.

1. iéuqn   _____
2. rpo uéq   _____
3. uácndo   _____
4. ónded   _____
5. mocó   _____

Proyecto
Work in pairs. Make up a question-answer game. It can be about sports, music, famous
people, Hollywood stars, etc. Include 20 questions-answers. Write the *interrogativas* in
Spanish. Example: *¿Quién* is the president? You can write the other words in English if you
do not know them in Spanish. Exchange questions with another group when finished. Play
the game in pairs or with the entire class.

Enrichment - Dibujemos
Draw a picture of five of your favorite Hollywood movie stars. Next to the picture, include a
question in Spanish about the stars. Example - *¿Dónde está Julia Roberts?*

11 - La familia

Name: _____

Date: _____

Class: _____

Vocabulario
Read and say the following family vocabulary out loud and in Spanish with your teacher .

el padre - father	**la madre-** mother
el hermano - brother	**la hermana** - sister
el abuelo - grandfather	**la abuela** - grandmother
el tío - uncle	**la tía** - aunt
el primo - cousin	**la prima** - cousin
el hijo - son	**la hija** - daughter
el esposo - husband	**la esposa** - wife
el cuñado - brother-in-law	**la cuñada** - sister-in-law
el yerno - son-in-law	**la nuera** - daughter-in-law

Sopa de Letras
With a classmate, find and circle the Spanish words listed below.

```
Y L Z P X I I E B E T P E L E L S A D S
A S O P S E A L L Q P L M A L U A I G Z
H C H D Y J K R A P E X I M A B T T D Q
M L C W A X I L E S A A Y A B V F F Í F
V C J Q A Ñ C K P U I D V D U P O L C A
E W O Q M I U O A O N S R R E W P K Q Z
E G J S G A S C A Q B A Y E L E N K H N
S L I I A O T B L U G N L U O T U R Y R
E L H D S Q P N J E A M I R P A L N M G
F Y L Q C C F J I H E W U H I G J M H D
Q F E S G R H C K I J I T K V X F O Z Y
E E A E Z I A S O M E V W A B C E L N K
K L P T A Y L E Y W I L D E E G A B G N
G O H L A H E R M A N A M L B C S E P W
P C K E W M U E H D Ñ G Y O I A Q Y W F
T R U P R T B O Q U V E W C J Q Z F X Z
E L T Í O M A Y C K R H M I Z Z L E J O
X O H S W R A A F N N F H S D C O Q M P
N N Y I H L L N O R C A P F T V O C A O
F V U M B X G J O E L P R I M O S Z V G
```

EL ABUELO
EL CUÑADO
EL ESPOSO
EL HERMANO
EL HIJO
EL PADRE
EL PRIMO
EL TÍO
EL YERNO
LA ABUELA
LA CUÑADA
LA ESPOSA
LA HERMANA
LA HIJA
LA MADRE
LA NUERA
LA PRIMA
LA TÍA

A
ALSOP

31

11 - La familia

Name: _____

Date: _____

Class: _____

Conversación

With a classmate, read and say the following dialogue between two students talking about their families.

Ernesto:	Gabriela, ¿cuántos (*how many*) hermanos tienes (*do you have*)?
Gabriela:	Tengo (*I have*) dos hermanos y una hermana.
Ernesto:	¿Tienes muchos primos?
Gabriela:	Pues, sí, tengo doce.
Ernesto:	¿Tienes tíos?
Gabriela:	Sí, tengo dos tíos y dos tías.
Ernesto:	¿Cómo se llaman (*what are the names*) tus padres?
Gabriela:	Jaime y Pilar.
Ernesto:	Tienes muchos parientes (*relatives*).

Teatro

With a classmate, role play that you are with a new acquaintance at school. Write a short conversation between the two of you. Find out about his/her family. Act out in front of the class. Include vocabulary from the **Vocabulario** and **Conversación** sections.

_____

_____

_____

_____

_____

_____

Interview a classmate. Find out about his/her family. Write a short conversation. Act out in front of the class. Include vocabulary from the **Vocabulario** and **Conversación** sections.

_____

_____

_____

_____

_____

11 - La familia

Name: _____

Date: _____

Class: _____

Juego
With a classmate, write in the missing letters.

1. y__r__o
2. t__o
3. p__i__a
4. h__rm__ __a
5. h__ __a
6. m__d__e
7. e__p__ __o
8. c__ñ__ __a
9. h__r__a__o
10. a__u__ __a

Proyecto
Work in pairs. Practice drawing your family members in the space below. Label in Spanish. Draw on a poster board when finished below. Make the drawings crazy!!!

Enrichment - internet
Find a Web site that includes Spanish vocabulary on the family. List the Web site address and the words you found in Spanish.

_____
_____
_____
_____
_____
_____

ALSOP

12 - El cuerpo

Name: _____

Date: _____

Class: _____

Vocabulario
Read and say the following words out loud and in Spanish with your teacher.

la cabeza - head
la nariz - nose
la oreja - ear
el estómago - stomach
la pierna - leg
los dedos - fingers
el oído - inner ear

el ojo - eye
la boca - mouth
el brazo - arm
la mano - hand
el pie - foot
la rodilla - knee

Across
2. eye
4. knee
5. nose
6. fingers
8. foot
9. leg
10. mouth

Down
1. arm
3. head
5. ear
6. hand
7. stomach

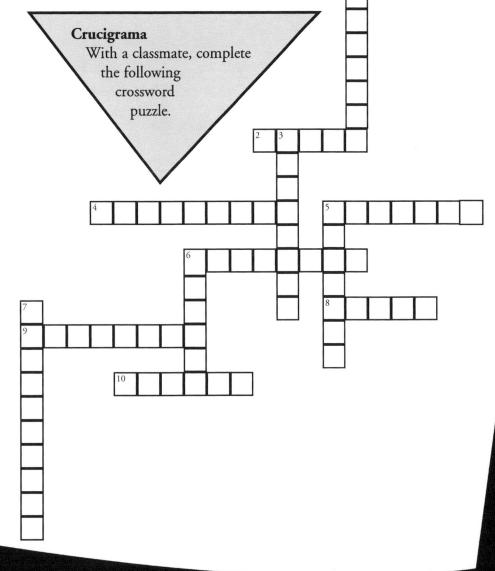

Crucigrama
With a classmate, complete the following crossword puzzle.

12 - El cuerpo

Name: _____

Date: _____

Class: _____

Conversación
With a classmate, read and say the following dialogue between the school nurse and a student.

Octavio:	Buenos días, Sra. Jiménez.
Sra. Jiménez:	Hola, Octavio. ¿Cómo estás?
Octavio:	No muy bien hoy, señora.
Sra. Jiménez:	¿Tienes dolor de estómago? (*Do you have a stomach ache?*)
Octavio:	No, tengo un dolor de cabeza.
Sra. Jiménez:	¿Hay otros síntomas?
Octavio:	Tengo un dolor de oído también.
Sra. Jiménez:	Pues, no tienes fiebre. (*Well, you don't have a fever.*) Por favor, descansa un rato. (*Please, rest a bit.*)
Octavio:	Gracias, señora.
Sra. Jiménez:	De nada (*You're welcome*), Octavio.

Teatro
With a classmate, role play that you are an ill patient and he/she is a doctor. Greet and tell the doctor how you are feeling. Answer his questions. Write a six-sentence conversation that takes place between the two of you. Include vocabulary from the **Vocabulario** and **Conversación** sections.

_____
_____
_____
_____
_____
_____

Convince your parents that you are sick and need to stay home from school today. Include vocabulary from the **Vocabulario** and **Conversación** sections.

_____
_____
_____
_____
_____

ALSOP

35

12 - El cuerpo

Name: _____

Date: _____

Class: _____

Juego
With a classmate, unscramble these Spanish words
and then give the meaning in English.

1. robza   _____
2. eraoj   _____
3. caob   _____
4. lodalir   _____
5. baceza   _____
6. osedd   _____
7. rzani   _____
8. eparni   _____
9. getamoso   _____
10. oman   _____

Proyecto
Make a puppet out of paper or heavy card stock. Paste each body part together labeling each
one in Spanish. Add some colorful clothes! Give your puppet a Spanish name. When
finished, introduce your puppet to the class!

Enrichment - Dibujemos
Draw a funny-looking alien from another planet. Label the body parts in Spanish. Add
color.

13 - Los cuartos de la casa

Name: _____

Date: _____

Class: _____

Vocabulario
Read and say the following rooms of the house out loud and in Spanish with your teacher.

la sala - living room
la alcoba - bedroom
el desván - attic
el sótano - basement
el comedor - dining room
el cuarto - room

la cocina - kitchen
el cuarto de baño - bathroom
la sala de estar - family room
la despensa - pantry
el garaje - garage
la casa - house

Sopa de Letras
Find and circle the following Spanish words.

```
E D E Q R J G L K K O A M Q Z J V Q X R
R B I L W O I T G D B J H X R N M E Q W
F E R N C B D K W O U Z P O B E H L B D
O M W Y T U E E C A L A S A L S A C C S
N L D B Y N A L M E L G A R A J E U L R
A F N E X G A R L O I A L U X C A A Z P
T G Z E E A Z M T L C A S N B Y C R E M
Ó E A L L W S T S O S L S A M O Q T W G
S C K D X J R H O A P F E X C H Z O U O
L L L E C T W H L F T C G I Q A Q D D G
E N N S C C G A W R P C N J F Z L E I W
Q J K V I C D N Q S H A F S F S H B Y Q
M H J Á G E X I L N B H O P T V I A J O
H P S N E G J F V M D N A R P Q Q Ñ A Y
O I C S R R H J M Q H A T G J H Y O X B
S P T V Z S F E N S V U P B K O B M S Z
C A V L U Y U M D S E N U U F W O D G O
R F D Q Q L I V V Z X V D J V T G P X V
P A J L C V I O V A S N E P S E D A L K
E K J E H G T O V R I H G X P X K L B O
```

EL COMEDOR
EL CUARTO
EL CUARTO DE BAÑO
EL DESVÁN
EL GARAJE
EL SÓTANO
LA ALCOBA
LA CASA
LA COCINA
LA DESPENSA
LA SALA
LA SALA DE ESTAR

ALSOP

37

13 - Los cuartos de la casa

Name: _____

Date: _____

Class: _____

Conversación

With a classmate, read and say the following dialogue between two students talking about their houses.

Concha:	Pepe, ¿cómo es tu casa (*what is your house like*)?
Pepe:	Pues, es una casa grande (*big*). Hay nueve cuartos.
Concha:	¿Hay (*is there*) comedor?
Pepe:	Sí, hay (*there is*) comedor y cocina.
Concha:	¿Hay sala?
Pepe:	Sí, hay sala.
Concha:	¿Hay sótano?
Pepe:	Pues sí. También hay desván.
Concha:	Pues tu casa es muy parecida (*similar*) a mi casa.

Teatro

With a classmate, role play that you are relatives talking about his/her new house. Write a short conversation between the two of you. Find out about his/her new house. Act out in front of the class. Include vocabulary from the **Vocabulario** and **Conversación** sections.

_____
_____
_____
_____
_____
_____

With a classmate, role play that you are telling a builder what kind of house you want. Use *quiero* (I want). Write a short conversation. Act out in front of the class. Include vocabulary from the **Vocabulario** and **Conversación** sections.

_____
_____
_____
_____
_____

ALSOP

13 - Los cuartos de la casa

Name: _____

Date: _____

Class: _____

Juego
With a classmate, write in the missing letters.

1. a__c__b__
2. c__a__t__ d__ b__ __o
3. __a__a
4. c__m__ __o__
5. __o__i__a
6. s__t__ __o
7. d__s__á__
8. __a__a__e
9. s__l__ d__ e__t__r
10. c__a__t__

Proyecto
Work in pairs. Practice drawing the rooms of your house in the space below. Label in Spanish. Make the drawings zany!!!

Enrichment - internet
Find Web sites which include information on *La Casa Rosada* in *Buenos Aires*. List the Web site address and some information on this famous house.

_____
_____
_____
_____
_____
_____

14 - Los dias y los meses

Name: _____

Date: _____

Class: _____

Vocabulario
Read and say the following words out loud and in Spanish with your teacher.

lunes - Monday
martes - Tuesday
miércoles - Wednesday
jueves - Thursday
viernes - Friday
sábado - Saturday
domingo - Sunday

enero - January
febrero - February
marzo - March
abril - April
mayo - May
junio - June
julio - July

agosto - August
septiembre - September
octubre - October
noviembre - November
diciembre - December

Crucigrama
With a classmate, complete the following crossword puzzle.

Across
4. Saturday
8. August
9. Sunday
11. June
12. January
13. April
14. Thursday
16. December
17. October
18. Friday

Down
1. Tuesday
2. February
3. Wednesday
5. Monday
6. March
7. November
10. May
14. July
15. September

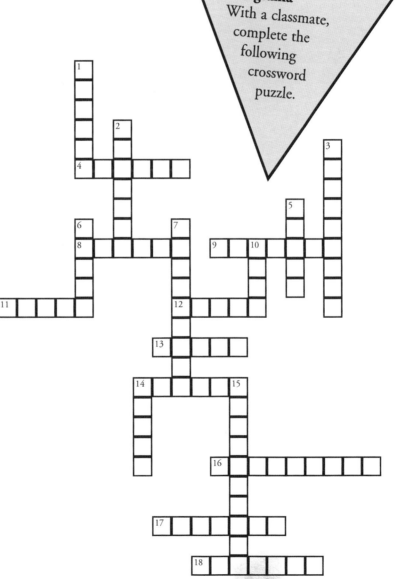

ALSOP

14 - Los dias y los meses

Name: _____

Date: _____

Class: _____

Conversación

With a classmate, read and say the following dialogue between two students in a school in New Mexico.

Rodrigo:	Hola, Ceci.
Ceci:	Hola, Rodrigo. ¿Cómo estás?
Rodrigo:	Bien, gracias. ¿Y tú?
Ceci:	Excelente. Rodrigo, ¿Qué día es hoy(*What day is today*)?
Rodrigo:	Es martes. ¿Por qué (*Why*)?
Ceci:	Miércoles es mi cumpleaños (*birthday*).
Rodrigo:	Mi cumpleaños es el cinco de enero.
Ceci:	Ah, es un viernes.
Rodrigo:	Sí, bueno, feliz cumpleaños (*happy birthday*), Ceci.
Ceci:	Gracias, Rodrigo. Adiós.

Teatro

Create a conversation with a classmate in which you tell each other when your birthdays take place. Write a six-sentence conversation that takes place between the two of you. Include vocabulary from the **Vocabulario** and **Conversación** sections.

_____

_____

_____

_____

_____

_____

With a classmate, role play that you are trying to set a dentist appointment (*una cita*) over the phone. Write a conversation between you and the receptionist. Discuss several days and dates and then finalize the appointment. Include vocabulary from the **Vocabulario** and **Conversación** sections.

_____

_____

_____

_____

_____

14 - Los dias y los meses

Juego
With a classmate, unscramble these Spanish words
and then give the meaning in English.

1. tasoog   _____
2. asdoba   _____
3. omzar   _____
4. satrem   _____
5. mogindo   _____
6. obrefer   _____
7. sujvee   _____
8. cbureto   _____
9. limocesre   _____
10. ibedecimr   _____

Proyecto
You have been choosen to design a calendar for the new year!!! In groups of three, make a
page for each month of the year. Label in Spanish the months and days of the week. Add
some decorations/drawings on each page. Use color. If you are really creative, design a cover
for your calendar!

Enrichment - Dibujemos
Draw a scene representing each of the four seasons. Then label the months in Spanish that
are associated with each season.

15 - El verbo ser

Frases con ser
Read and say the following words out loud and in Spanish with your teacher.

1. **Juana es médica.**
2. **Elena es profesora.**
3. **Diego es de España.**
4. **Soy** (*I am*) **de México.**
5. **Esperanza es inteligente.**
6. **David es guapo** (*handsome*)

7. **soy**-I am
8. **eres**-you are
9. **es**-he, she is
10. **somos**-we are
11. **son**-they are

Sopa de Letras
With a classmate, find and circle the Spanish words listed below.

```
E R A A D R V Z V Y L D U H A E E Q S
U R Q N E S E S P A Ñ O L A R F S Q A J
O B E Q A K G G T I X E P E D I A W P N
G C H S G I F A V L J O S K N T C E A J
S O I G I L B C C X A G H T L B N S U U
F Q E D Y N O M J S U I E A U E V D G C
F D E H É E T V O A J L S A H S W E S A
I C K T L M W E P L I E W L L D V C E R
I Y G T C S S O L G O A I Q E E L H H O
K G J M L E J E N I T C G D S C F I H S
P S I V U E R T X S G G S C R O Q L R E
F N W E O A E E I V W E T E Z S Q E V F
E T N A I D U T S E S E N I I T T L U O
A K D X M Y N Z D B T L X T N A K M A R
N K O D O E H D R F O U Q R E R F H A P
C I Y E D N T W C W M N N S N I G L R S
Q H H S A N A B U C S E I L T C X W V E
P S E R N C R T A W U H T T Q A R F N E
X I B H V F Y F M C V E B C A R F I Q P
F G D N J F B M Q G Y A N L C R I T C C
```

ERES BONITA
ERES GUAPO
ERES INTELIGENTE
ES ALTA
ES COLOMBIANA
ES CUBANA
ES DE CHILE
ES DE COSTA RICA
ES DENTISTA
ES ESPAÑOLA
ES ESTUDIANTE
ES GUAPA
ES INTELIGENTE
ES MÉDICO
ES PROFESORA

15 - El verbo ser

Name: _____

Date: _____

Class: _____

Conversación
With a classmate, read and say the following dialogue between two university students using the verb "**ser**" (to be).

Chepina:	Carlos, ¿de dónde eres?
Carlos:	Soy de Costa Rica. ¿Y tú?
Chepina:	Soy de México. ¿Eres (*are you*) médico?
Carlos:	No, soy estudiante. ¿Y eres profesora?
Chepina:	No, también soy estudiante.
Carlos:	Eres muy bonita.
Chepina:	Gracias, Carlos. Eres muy guapo.
Carlos:	Gracias, Chepina.
Chepina:	Pues, tengo (*I have*) clase. Nos vemos mañana. (*We will see each other tomorrow.*)

Teatro
With a classmate, role play that you are having a conversation with a new student at school. Write a short conversation between the two of you. Find out where he/she is from. Find out what he/she is. Act out in front of the class. Include vocabulary from the **Frases con ser** and **Conversación** sections.

_____
_____
_____
_____
_____
_____

Work in pairs. Take turns describing each other. Use the verb *ser-eres*. Write the descriptions below. Act out in front of the class. Include vocabulary from the **Frases con ser** and **Conversación** sections

_____
_____
_____
_____
_____
_____

15 - El verbo ser

Name: _____

Date: _____

Class: _____

Juego
Write in the missing letters to complete the following Spanish words.

1. e__e__
2. e__
3. s__y
4. g__a__o
5. a__ __a
6. b__n__ __a
7. i__t__l__g__nt__
8. e__p__ñ__l__
9. c__b__ __o
10. __é__ i__a

Proyecto
Work in pairs. Practice drawing three pictures of yourself. Label in Spanish using the verb *ser*. Example-*Soy alto*-I am tall, *Soy alumno(a)*. Put your drawings on poster board for an art exhibit in your class.

Enrichment - internet
Find a Web site that includes information about the uses of the verb *ser*. List the Web site address and some information you found at the site. Use Spanish grammar as the key words for your search.

_____
_____
_____
_____
_____
_____
_____

16 - El verbo estar

Name: _____

Date: _____

Class: _____

Frases con estar
Read and say the following sentences out loud and in Spanish with your teacher.

1. **Salvador está en México.**
2. **Estás** (*you are*) **enfermo(a)** (*sick*).
3. **Marisela está en España.**
4. **Estoy cansado(a)** (*tired*).
5. **estoy** - I am
6. **estás** - you are
7. **está** - he, she is
8. **estamos** - we are
9. **están** - they are
10. **Lucero está contenta.**
11. **Guillermo está triste (sad).**
12. **¿Cómo estás?**
13. **Estoy bien.**

Crucigrama
With a classmate, complete the following crossword puzzle.

Across
6. He is happy.

Down
1. How are you?
2. You are sick.
3. I am fine.
4. I am tired.
5. He is in Mexico.
6. He is sad.

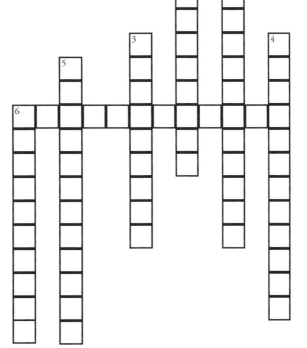

16 - El verbo estar

Name: _____

Date: _____

Class: _____

Conversación

With a classmate, read and say the following dialogue between two friends who are chatting in a local café.

Beatriz:	Rodrigo, ¿cómo estás?
Rodrigo:	Bien, ¿y tú?
Beatriz:	Estoy enferma. Tengo catarro (*a cold*).
Rodrigo:	Pobrecita. Y tu hermana María, ¿está en España?
Beatriz:	Sí, está en Madrid.
Rodrigo:	Yo estoy aquí, en Detroit.
Beatriz:	¿Cómo está tu novia?
Rodrigo:	Bien, está muy contenta.
Beatriz:	Pues, Rodrigo, tengo que irme (*I have to leave*), adiós.
Rodrigo:	Adiós, Beatriz. Hasta luego.

Teatro

Work with a classmate. Write a short conversation between the two of you. Find out how he/she is. Ask where his/her boyfriend/girlfriend is. Act out in front of the class. Include vocabulary from the **Frases con estar** and **Conversación** sections.

_____
_____
_____
_____
_____
_____

Work in pairs. Role play two Hollywood stars. Use the verb "*estar*". Find out how each is and where each is located. Act out in front of the class. Include vocabulary from the **Frases con estar** and **Conversación** sections.

_____
_____
_____
_____
_____

ALSOP

47

16 - El verbo estar

Name: _____

Date: _____

Class: _____

Juego
Write in the missing letters to complete the following Spanish words.

1. e__t__s
2. e__t__y
3. e__t__
4. c__m__
5. e__
6. E__p__ñ__
7. M__x__c__
8. c__n__a__o
9. t__i__t__
10. e__f__r__o

Proyecto
Work in pairs. Write an ad for a new book called *¿Dónde está Jaime?* Include where *Jaime* (Jim) is in the book. Example: *Jaime está en México.* List eight places where *Jaime* is.

Enrichment - Dibujemos
Draw below three famous people. Say how they are and where they are.

17 - El verbo tener

Name: _____

Date: _____

Class: _____

Vocabulario
Read and say the following words out loud and in Spanish with your teacher.

tengo - I have
tienes - you have
tiene - he,she has
tenemos - we have
tienen - they have
la bandera - flag

la mochila - book bag
el drama - play
el escritorio - desk
la silla - chair
viejo, a - old
¿qué tal? - how's everything?

Sopa de Letras
Find and circle the Spanish words listed below.

```
D F S L A B R R P V E H U T O A L H N G
V T O F Y R Y S P K Y V I N F L X Y G Y
E A P M E N E Q V W O E S K D I B N G V
I T V U V O T D A D N T C N H H U S V G
J T K Q D U R X N E M U U I Y C O M T M
J W J E K V S F N A A C A C D O H I E H
W K N Q N O X J V T B Z M V V M O G Y I
V K X L M E K C Z G N A Q Y S A K I V H
B L Q E Q X I P I K E J L H C L R B X V
E O N M A E H T I O I E O M H X X N G G
P E Q O L P O I R O T I R C S E L E A N
T K R L R V U A N Y U V H E Z F Q I E P
S S D O M L B V C V N T I J P T B C T N
T L H A N U Z X F A P H S V N U V D Y M
I Q A Y B Y H D D Y X S I X U D J J V W
E S U S I M X M V P Z Y I L O K X H Q L
N D O C I G W I P K H X P U H R I S I F
E X K E J L O G N E T U C E L D R A M A
S F Y E T D L Z X L U X I O K I S Y W N
S G I Y A U J A E Q J U S V O G T W C T
```

EL DRAMA
EL ESCRITORIO
LA BANDERA
LA MOCHILA
LA SILLA
TENEMOS
TENGO
TIENE
TIENEN
TIENES
VIEJA

ALSOP

17 - El verbo tener

Conversación

With a classmate, read and say the following dialogue between Tere and Rafa. They are discussing the props they have for the school play.

Tere: Hola, Rafa.

Rafa: Hola, Tere. ¿Qué tal?

Tere: Muy bien, gracias.

Rafa: Tere, ¿tienes (*do you have*) una mochila para el drama?

Tere: Si, tengo dos mochilas.

Rafa: Bueno, y tengo una calculadora y una regla.

Tere: ¿Tienes una bandera?

Rafa: Si, tengo una bandera pero (*but*) es vieja.

Tere: Esta bien. (*It's OK*). Tengo una silla.

Rafa: Excelente. Es todo.(*That's all*)

Tere: Adiós, Rafa.

Rafa: Hasta pronto, Tere.

Teatro

With a classmate, make up a conversation between two people discussing the props they have for a school play. Write a six-sentence conversation that takes place between the two of you. Include vocabulary from the **Vocabulario** and **Conversación** sections.

_____

_____

_____

_____

_____

_____

Create a six-sentence conversation between two friends planning a birthday party. Discuss items they each have for the party. (Hint: *invitación*, *refrescos*, *decoraciones*, *platos*, *globos*) Include vocabulary from the **Vocabulario** and **Conversación** sections.

_____

_____

_____

_____

_____

ALSOP

50

17 - El verbo tener

Name: _____

Date: _____

Class: _____

Juego
With a classmate, unscramble the following words and give the English meaning.

1. radma _____
2. nitee _____
3. lsali _____
4. genot _____
5. renabad _____
6. jiave _____
7. osetiricor _____
8. semoten _____
9. clihoma _____
10. ensite _____

Proyecto
With a classmate, create a mobile of some of the favorite things you each have at home. Use the verb *tenemos* for we have. On each item (a drawing or picture), write a sentence in Spanish. (Example: *Tenemos un perro.* We have a dog.)

Enrichment - Dibujemos
Draw a minimum of eight items you have at home. Color them interesting colors. Use a Spanish dictionary for new words. Under each picture, write a Spanish sentence telling what you have. (Example: *Tengo tres teléfonos.* I have three telephones.)

ALSOP

18 - El verbo ir

Name: _____

Date: _____

Class: _____

Frases con ir
Read and say the following sentences out loud
and in Spanish with your teacher.

1. **¿Adónde vas?** (Where are you going?)
2. **Voy a Sevilla.** (I am going to Sevilla.)
3. **¿Vas a casa?** (Are you going home?)
4. **Sí, voy a casa.** (Yes, I am going home.)
5. **voy** - I go, am going
6. **vas** - you go
7. **va** - he, she goes
8. **vamos** - we go
9. **van** - they go

Crucigrama
With a classmate, complete
the following
crossword puzzle.

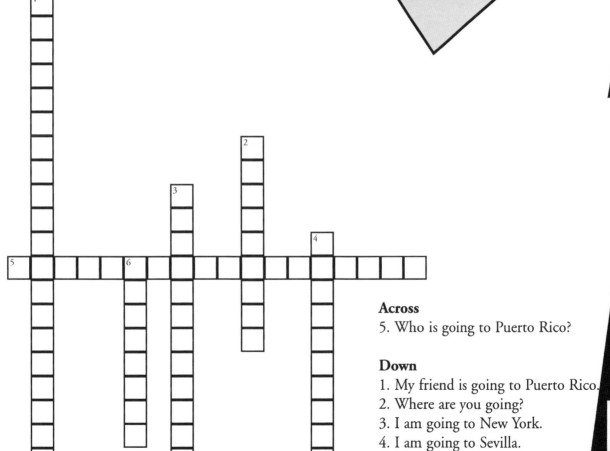

Across
5. Who is going to Puerto Rico?

Down
1. My friend is going to Puerto Rico.
2. Where are you going?
3. I am going to New York.
4. I am going to Sevilla.
6. Are you going home?

18 - El verbo ir

Conversación

With a classmate, read and say the following dialogue between a husband and wife.

Pancho:	Rocío, ¿adónde vas?
Rocío:	Voy a la casa de mi amiga.
Pancho:	Voy al partido de fútbol (*soccer game*).
Rocío:	¿No vas al banco? (*bank*)
Pancho:	No, hoy no está abierto (*open*).
Rocío:	Vamos (*we are going*) al cine (*movie*).
Pancho:	¿Vas mañana a la iglesia? (*church*)
Rocío:	Pues, sí. Voy porque (*because*) es domingo (*Sunday*).
Pancho:	Pues, que te diviertas (*have a good time*).
Rocío:	Adiós, Pancho. Hasta luego.

Teatro

With a classmate, write a short conversation between the two of you. Find out where he/she is going. Act out in front of the class. Include vocabulary from the **Frases con ir** and **Conversación** sections.

_____
_____
_____
_____
_____
_____

Work in pairs. Role play two teachers talking about their summer vacation. Use the verb *ir*. They ask where each is going. Act out in front of the class. Include vocabulary from the **Frases con ir** and **Conversación** sections.

_____
_____
_____
_____
_____

18 - El verbo ir

Name: _____

Date: _____

Class: _____

Juego
Write in the missing letters to complete the
following Spanish words.

1. d__n__e
2. v__s
3. v__y
4. q__i__n
5. B__r__e__o__a
6. P__e__t__ R__c__
7. M__x__c__
8. S__v__ll__

Proyecto
Work in pairs. Make a list of famous people. Say where each is going on vacation. Use your
list in a Hollywood gossip magazine.

Enrichment - Dibujemos
Draw below three of your relatives. Label them in Spanish and list where each is going.
Example-*Mi tío va a Cancún.*

www.teachersdiscovery.com

19 - La comida

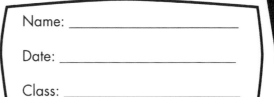

Name: _____

Date: _____

Class: _____

Vocabulario
Read and say the following words out loud and in Spanish with your teacher.

1. **la hamburguesa** - hamburger
2. **las papas fritas** - French fries
3. **la carne** - meat
4. **el perro caliente** - hot dog
5. **la leche** - milk
6. **el café** - coffee
7. **el postre** - dessert
8. **la fruta** - fruit
9. **las legumbres** - vegetables
10. **la ensalada** - salad
11. **el helado** - ice cream
12. **el pan** - bread
13. **el pollo** - chicken

Sopa de Letras
With a classmate, find and circle the following Spanish words.

```
E L X B R Y I N L E L Z E Y Y M O A S E
N L A U R V J D A G A K R N Z D W C L S
O S P L M D X E F B S U T B S K T P H C
P S Z E E F R H R B P V S P K G O Z O I
D X A Y R C Z R U W A K O R S L V D U C
U N Y D V R H F T T P B P L L Y A B R F
A B G X A W O E A Y A S L O W L G Z G L
L F S S H L F C A N S Z E Q E M P X A U
Q R H D K F A M A C F W W H O F W H J X
U O C I Z X M S G L R Z L S Y K A I P V
J T Q S D Q X F N O I E M D M M Z T X O
T R Q B Q G L B P E T E A C B L P T D C
S E R B M U G E L S A L N U N V X H Y R
K T W V L S F Q S V S L R T H A J S M O
C H Z R C L C Z S L E G Y G E A P L V W
Q K R J F S V W D U U K Z O R Q E L S F
B U K T G D R L V E P Z P J L K P X E P
C M P P C R P B S K L A C A R N E V E G
C D E U B É F A C L E S N X N H G P E G
N I O V E U I J E Z F I R R Z Z B S Q U
```

EL CAFÉ
EL HELADO
EL PAN
EL PERRO
CALIENTE
EL POLLO
EL POSTRE
LA CARNE
LA ENSALADA
LA FRUTA
LA HAMBURGUESA
LA LECHE
LAS LEGUMBRES
LAS PAPAS FRITAS

19 - La comida

Name: _____

Date: _____

Class: _____

Conversación
With a classmate, read and say the following dialogue between two students in the school cafeteria.

Andrés: Hola, Adriana. ¿Cómo estás?

Adriana: Así-así, Andrés. Gracias.

Andrés: ¿Qué hay para comer (*What is there to eat*)?

Adriana: Hay (*There is*) hamburguesas o perros calientes.

Andrés: Quiero (*I prefer*)una hamburguesa. ¿Y tú?

Adriana: Quiero un perro caliente.

Andrés: También (*Also*) hay fruta o legumbres, ¿verdad (*right*)?

Adriana: Sí, Andrés. Hoy quiero (*Today I want*) un postre.

Andrés: Yo quiero leche.

Adriana: ¡Buen provecho (*Enjoy your meal*)!

Teatro
Imagine that your family is visiting a new diner. Write a six-sentence conversation that takes place among the family. Include vocabulary from the **Vocabulario** and **Conversación** sections.

_____
_____
_____
_____
_____
_____

With a classmate, role play that you are the owner of a neighborhood restaurant and he/she is the head chef. Discuss the food being prepared for the menu this evening. Write a six-sentence conversation that takes place between the two of you. Include vocabulary from the **Vocabulario** and **Conversación** sections.

_____
_____
_____
_____
_____

19 - La comida

Juego
With a classmate, write in the missing letters of the Spanish words below, and give the English meaning.

1. po_tr_   _____
2. _ec_e   _____
3. en_a_ada   _____
4. c_rne   _____
5. fr_t_   _____
6. l_gum_res   _____
7. _apas f_itas   _____
8. c_f_   _____
9. p_rro ca_ien_e _____
10. ha_bur_uesa   _____

Proyecto
In a group of three, plan a menu for a Mexican restaurant. Design a cover and create a name for the restaurant. Include 12 food choices in your menu. Write in prices in pesos (Mexico).
Hint: 11 pesos = $1

Enrichment - internet
Find a Web site for a Mexican or Spanish restaurant. Tell the name of the restaurant and add eight additional foods, in Spanish, that you found at that site.

_____
_____
_____
_____
_____
_____
_____

20 - Los sustantivos/adjetivos

Name: _____

Date: _____

Class: _____

Frases con los sustantivos/adjetivos
Read and say the following sentences out loud and in Spanish with your teacher.

1. **El chico es guapo.** (The boy is handsome.)
2. **Los chicos son guapos.** (The boys are handsome.)
3. **La chica es bonita**. (The girl is pretty.)
4. **Las chicas son bonitas.** (The girls are pretty.)
5. **José es alto** (tall).
6. **María es alta** (tall).
7. **Los chicos son altos.**
8. **Las chicas son altas.**

Crucigrama
With a classmate, complete the following crossword puzzle.

Across
3. The boy is handsome.
5. The boys are handsome.
7. Joe is tall.

Down
1. The girl is pretty.
2. The girls are pretty.
4. Mary is tall.
6. The boys are tall.

20 - Los sustantivos/adjetivos

Name: _____

Date: _____

Class: _____

Conversación
With a classmate, read and say the following dialogue between a brother and his sister.

Matilde:	Eduardo, tu novia es muy bonita.
Eduardo:	Y tu novio es muy guapo.
Matilde:	Y tu amigo Arturo, es muy alto.
Eduardo:	Sí, juega (*he plays*) en el equipo (*team*) de baloncesto (*basketball*).
Matilde:	Pues, mi amiga Mariluz es muy alta.
Eduardo:	Y también (*also*) juega al baloncesto.
Matilde:	Me gusta (*I like*) la casa de Mariluz. Es muy bonita.
Eduardo:	Pues, tengo que salir (*I have to leave*) para la escuela.
Matilde:	Bien, que te diviertas (*have a good time*).
Eduardo:	Gracias, adiós. Hasta luego.

Teatro
Work with a classmate. Write a short conversation between the two of you. You describe your boyfriends/girlfriends and their houses. Include vocabulary from the **Frases con los sustantivos/adjetivos** and **Conversación** sections.

_____
_____
_____
_____
_____
_____

Work in pairs. Role play a mother and father talking about their children. Use three nouns and adjectives. Act out in front of the class. Include vocabulary from the **Frases con los sustantivos/adjetivos** and **Conversación** sections.

_____
_____
_____
_____
_____

A
ALSOP

59

20 - Los sustantivos/adjetivos

Name: _____

Date: _____

Class: _____

Juego
Write in the missing letters to complete the following Spanish words.

1. c__s__s
2. l__s
3. s__n
4. b__n__t__s
5. __l
6. e_
7. c_i_o
8. g_a_o
9. a_ t _ s

Proyecto
Work in pairs. Make a list of four of your friends in Spanish class. Describe them with an adjective in Spanish. Include the list in a class newspaper describing your friends. Make a small drawing of each friend.

Enrichment - Dibujemos
Draw below a boy or girl. Label them in Spanish using a noun/adjective for each of them. Example - *El chico es rico* (rich). Enter your drawing in the Salvador Dali art exhibit. Make your drawings zany!

Parte Dos-Cultura

La geografía
Tú-usted
Los abrazos y los besos
La corrida de toros
El fútbol
La Navidad
El Día de los Muertos
La comida mexicana
La comida española
La música latina
Los animales
Los pintores
Los escritores

21 - La geografía

Name: _____

Date: _____

Class: _____

Hechos Importantes
Read and say the following capital cities-countries
out loud and in Spanish with your teacher.

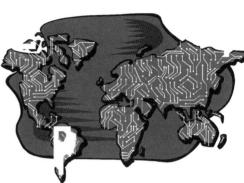

La Ciudad de México-México   San José-Costa Rica
La Habana-Cuba   San Juan-Puerto Rico
Managua-Nicaragua   Bogotá-Colombia
Caracas-Venezuela   Quito-Ecuador
Lima-Perú   Santiago-Chile
Buenos Aires-Argentina   Montevideo-Uruguay
Asunción-Paraguay   Sucre, La Paz-Bolivia

Sopa de Letras
With a classmate, find and circle the listed
cities and countries.

```
B T Z A L E U Z E N E V K G Ú A Z N O C
A U Z C O L O M B I A N T O Ñ R Ó W G P
K Y E B K A G Y I C T A Y A Z I E Q A Y
I O P N E O L O Q A C D P A C N V P I O
U R L Z O C K M K R P S Q N U P V A T H
C W D F E S E P N A E O U R L G R B N A
H V M E C V A Q H E G Á S H Y Z G A D A J
H M G K U M P I K U A T V P E E A R S K
C B M H A D I H R A Z Q O N I I F B A L
T A S J D B U D R E T E T G U O O X I P
T R R O O S W U C S S I J G O L I C L B
N S C A R X A U G A N A M Y I B Y H F K
Q Y P O C S G S G A Z P O V M É X I C O
S U P X H A U O H I R V I M A C D L X Z
T W I Z I C S D I R E A Y D K S L E O W
P F J T R A M I L I S V W V I U T D V H
M P Q E O J X R O K K A T M Q E B Q D E
S X X D G B G D D K R N G N D W B U O M
C J U X S C B A T D B S P V S W Z B C A
A R I F W H O M V Q M R N P N V M P B V
```

ARGENTINA
ASUNCIÓN
BOGOTÁ
BOLIVIA
BUENOS AIRES
CARACAS
CHILE
COLOMBIA
ECUADOR
ESPAÑA
LIMA
MADRID
MANAGUA
MÉXICO
NICARAGUA
PARAGUAY
PERÚ
QUITO
SANTIAGO
SUCRE
VENEZUELA

www.teachersdiscovery.com

A ALSOP

21 - La geografía

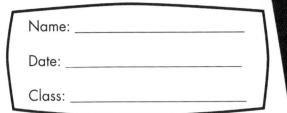

Name: _____

Date: _____

Class: _____

Conversación

With a classmate, read and say the following dialogue between two students from Spanish-speaking countries.

Estela:	Hola, ¿cómo te llamas?
Daniel:	Me llamo Daniel. ¿Y tú, cómo te llamas?
Estela:	Me llamo Estela. ¿De dónde eres?
Daniel:	Soy de México. ¿Y tú?
Estela:	Soy de Puerto Rico.
Daniel:	Pues, mucho gusto.
Estela:	El gusto es mío.
Daniel:	Adiós.
Estela:	Adiós. Hasta luego.

Teatro

With a classmate, role play that you are meeting a student in your school from Ecuador. Write a short conversation between the two of you. Find out where he/she is from. Act out in front of the class. Include vocabulary from the **Hechos Importantes** and **Conversación** sections.

_____

_____

_____

_____

_____

_____

With a classmate, role play that you are at a Mexican restaurant, speaking with a waitress. Introduce yourself and find out where the waitress is from. Write a short conversation. Act out in front of the class. Include vocabulary from the **Hechos Importantes** and **Conversación** sections.

_____

_____

_____

_____

_____

21 - La geografía

Name: _____

Date: _____

Class: _____

Juego
Write in the missing letters to complete the following country names.

1. B__g__tá, C__l__mb__a
2. M__n__gu__, N__c__r__g__a
3. B__e__o__ A__r__s, A__g__n__i__a
4. M__d__i__, E__p__ñ__
5. C__r__c__, __en__ __ue __ __
6. __an __u__n, __ue__t__ __ic__
7. __a __iu__a__ d__ __é__ic__
8. __uc__e, __o__i__ia
9. __u__t__, __cu__d__r
10. __a__t__ag__ , __hi__e

Proyecto
Work in pairs. Draw and label a map of Spain, Mexico, Central and South America. Write the names of the countries and capitals. Draw on a poster board.

Enrichment - internet
List below the Web site addresses for three countries where Spanish is spoken. Include a summary sentence of information found for each. Include locations, weather, and some important cities, bodies of water, etc.

_____
_____
_____
_____
_____
_____
_____
_____

22 - Tú-usted

Name: _____

Date: _____

Class: _____

Hechos Importantes

Read and say the following sentences out loud and in Spanish with your teacher.

1. **Hola, Juan, ¿cómo estás?** (*How are you?*)
2. **Hola, señor, ¿cómo está usted?**
3. **¿Estudias español?** (*Do you study Spanish?*)
4. **¿Estudia usted (Ud.) español?**
5. **¿Dónde vives?** (*Where do you live?*)
6. **¿Dónde vive usted (Ud.)?**
7. **¿Adónde vas?** (*Where are you going?*)
8. **¿Adónde va usted (Ud.)?**

In Spanish, there are two ways to say "you:" "*tú*" or "*usted*". The *tú* form is the familiar way to say "you." It is used with friends and family. The *usted* form is the formal or polite way to say "you." It is used with people you first meet and people you do not know well.

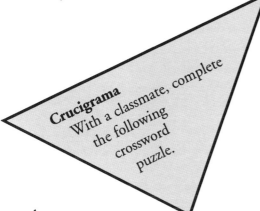

Crucigrama
With a classmate, complete the following crossword puzzle.

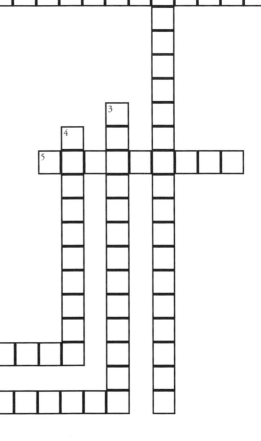

Across
2. Do you (familiar) study Spanish?
5. How are you (familiar)?
6. Where are you (familiar) going?
7. Where do you (formal) live?

Down
1. Do you (formal) study Spanish?
3. Where are you (formal) going?
4. Where do you (familiar) live?

ALSOP

22 - Tú-usted

Name: _____

Date: _____

Class: _____

Conversación
Working with a classmate, read and say the following dialogue between two friends.

Maribel:	Julio, buenos días, ¿cómo estás?
Julio:	Bien, ¿y tú?
Maribel:	Muy bien. ¿Vas al concierto?
Julio:	Sí, ¿y vas tú?
Maribel:	Sí, voy a ir.
Julio:	¿Cuándo vas?
Maribel:	Voy (*I am going*) en dos días. ¿Y tú?
Julio:	Voy en cinco días.
Maribel:	Pues, que te diviertas (*have a good time*).
Julio:	Gracias, Maribel. Adiós. Hasta luego.

Teatro
Work with a classmate. Write a short conversation between the two of you. Find out where he/she is going. Act out in front of the class. Include vocabulary from the **Hechos Importantes** and **Conversación** sections.

_____
_____
_____
_____
_____
_____

Work in pairs. You meet someone in the street. Greet the person and ask how he/she is and where he/she lives. Use the formal/polite "*usted*" form. Act out in front of the class. Include vocabulary from the **Hechos Importantes** and **Conversación** sections.

_____
_____
_____
_____
_____

22 - Tú-usted

Name: _____

Date: _____

Class: _____

Juego

Write in the missing letters to complete the following Spanish words.

1. e__t__s
2. e__t__
3. t__
4. u__t__d
5. v__s
6. v____e
7. v__v__s
8. d__n__e
9. e__t__d__ __s
10. v__

Proyecto

Work in pairs. Practice in the space below. Write your own explanation of the "*tú-usted*" ways to express "you" in Spanish.

Enrichment - Dibujemos

Draw below two friends talking in Spanish. Write two sentences of dialogue for each. Use the "*tú*" form. Draw below a meeting between you and a person in the street. Use the "*usted*"-formal/polite command in the dialogue. Include two questions and two answers.

23 - Los abrazos y los besos

Name: _____

Date: _____

Class: _____

Hechos Importantes
Let's practice some expressions and customs.

1. **Un abrazo** (*hug*)**, María.**
2. **Abrazos y besos** (*kisses*)**.**
3. **Recibe un fuerte abrazo.**
4. **Besos y abrazos.**
5. **Besos.**
6. **Abrazos.**

The Spanish custom of giving a person a hug and a kiss extends through many of the Latin American countries. When someone in Spain greets another, it is customary to show affection for that person by kissing each cheek. It is also customary to give a hug on greeting one another.

Sopa de Letras
With a classmate, find and circle the words listed below.

```
G Z C H Q X M Y O P F S O N X U G X I S
U J V X K C G A G J O K Z X S S G C I M
G K T P S E V Z Q Z C Q A G W J X O D I
X W H X I O L J A N D K R W J A N C W F
L F F E U A Z R P T W I B T P J U I I S
E D L F L E B A T F C M A I E J O S I A
O Z A R B A E T R E U F N U J E U K I G
T J A O A C L Z W B K E U Y W B K X I U
H J S R T T L B F X A W I S N R F N C F
D N Y I B G O L H A C Y T V F I T S B S
C R M O K I E W S C B W S X W W K O N E
Y X B I J Z R A W J J T R O V I Z V I I
Y K H N I O E D T M E E S T S H F Q Z O
T M P O B R E C I B E N D X E E K L J S
E J J Z U E F U A X L I R M P R B R S F
B A J L G I S C M M R H S V P U R V J K
K G M B G E O O U R I B L I S X A P K T
B B O V K O W Z S C E Z X R T O Q N L C
J O S K M I H E T B U T W F E I F D S D
Y A D Z E C Z J L E H G R E L N Z G I N
```

ABRAZOS
BESOS
BESOS Y ABRAZOS
RECIBE
UN ABRAZO
UN FUERTE ABRAZO

ALSOP
68

23 - Los abrazos y los besos

Name: _____

Date: _____

Class: _____

Conversación

With a classmate, read and say the following dialogue between two friends.

Fernando:	Isabel, ¿qué tal, cómo estás? (*Fernando kisses Isabel on both cheeks. The two hug*).
Isabel:	Bien, ¿y tú?
Fernando:	Bien.
Isabel:	¿Qué hay? (*What's new?*)
Fernando:	Pues, voy a estudiar en la universidad.
Isabel:	¿Cuándo empiezas?
Fernando:	El semestre que viene (*next semester*).
Isabel:	¿Qué vas a estudiar?
Fernando:	Medicina.
Isabel:	Pues, felicitaciones (*congratulations*). Ahora tengo que trabajar. (*I have to work*). Adiós. Hasta pronto.
Fernando:	Adiós. Te llamo esta noche. (*I'll call you tonight*).

Teatro

Work with a classmate. Role play that you meet an old friend of the family. Write a short conversation between the two of you. Find out how the other is and what's new. Give one another a hug and kisses. Act out in front of the class. Include vocabulary from the **Hechos Importantes** and **Conversación** sections.

_____
_____
_____
_____
_____
_____

Work in pairs. You meet a friend from school. Greet the person and ask how he/she is and what's new. Give one another a hug and kisses. Act out in front of the class. Include vocabulary from the **Hechos Importantes** and **Conversación** sections.

_____
_____
_____
_____
_____

A

ALSOP

69

23 - Los abrazos y los besos

Name: _____

Date: _____

Class: _____

Juego

With a classmate, unscramble the following Spanish words and give the meaning in English.

1. osbe _____
2. ozbaras _____
3. sbeos _____
4. ercbie _____
5. demciani _____
6. seáts _____
7. nibe _____
8. móco _____

Proyecto

Work in groups of four. Videotape a meeting between friends. Include a short conversation in Spanish as well as *abrazos* and *besos*. This is your chance to be a true "*estrella del cine!*"

Enrichment - Dibujemos

Draw a picture of two friends meeting. They hug and kiss one another on each cheek of the face. Label the drawing in Spanish!

24 - La corrida de toros

Name: _____

Date: _____

Class: _____

Hechos Importantes
Practice pronouncing the following bullfighting vocabulary out loud with your teacher.

Bullfights are a tradition in Spain. There are also bullfights in Mexico and some South American countries. Bullfights usually take place on Sunday afternoon. They often begin at five p.m. There are three bullfighters. Each will kill two bulls. There are six bulls killed in a two-hour bullfight.

la capa - cape
la muleta - small red cape
el picador - rider on horseback who sticks the bull with a lance
el banderillero - man who sticks barbed sticks into the bull's neck
el matador (torero) - the bullfighter, literally the "killer"
el estoque - the sword the bullfighter uses to kill the bull
los pases - passes done by the bullfighter with the cape
el toro - the bull

Crucigrama
With a classmate, complete the following crossword puzzle.

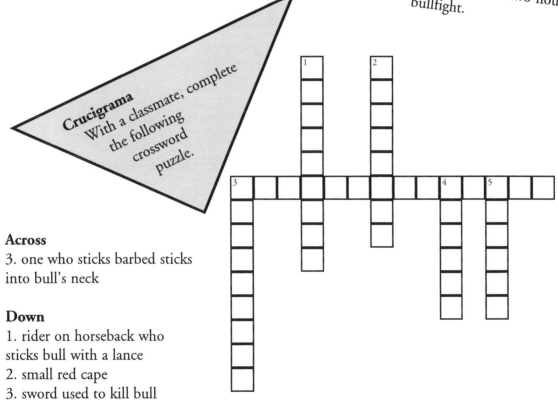

Across
3. one who sticks barbed sticks into bull's neck

Down
1. rider on horseback who sticks bull with a lance
2. small red cape
3. sword used to kill bull
4. cape
5. bull

ALSOP

24 - La corrida de toros

Name: _____

Date: _____

Class: _____

Conversación

With a classmate, read and say the following dialogue between two friends who talk about Ernesto's visit to the bullfight.

Paquita:	Ernesto, ¿vas (*are you going*) a la corrida de toros?
Ernesto:	Sí.
Paquita:	¿Cuándo vas?
Ernesto:	Este domingo.
Paquita:	¿A qué hora empieza (*begin*) la corrida?
Ernesto:	A las cinco. ¿Quieres (*do you want*) ir?
Paquita:	No, no me gusta (*I do not like*) la corrida de toros.
Ernesto:	¿Por qué?
Paquita:	No me gusta la violencia.
Ernesto:	Pues, me gusta la tradición de la corrida.
Paquita:	Pues, que te diviertas (*have a good time*). Adiós.
Ernesto:	Hasta luego, Paquita.

Teatro

Work with a classmate. Role play that you meet a famous bullfighter. Write a short conversation between the two of you. Find out the bullfighter's name and ask him about the bullfight. Act out in front of the class. Include vocabulary from the **Hechos Importantes** and **Conversación** sections.

_____

_____

_____

_____

_____

_____

Work in pairs. You talk with your teacher about the bullfight. Each of you say why you like (*me gusta*) or do not like (*no me gusta*) the bullfight. Act out in front of the class. Include vocabulary from the **Hechos Importantes** and **Conversación** sections.

_____

_____

_____

_____

_____

A

ALSOP

72

24 - La corrida de toros

Name: _____

Date: _____

Class: _____

Juego
Write in the missing letters to complete the following bullfighting words.

1. m__l__t__
2. c__p__
3. e__t__q__e
4. p__c__d__r
5. __a__a__o__
6. b__n__e__i__ __e__o
7. p__s__
8. t__r__

Proyecto
In the space below practice drawing the *picador*, the *banderillo* , and the *matador*. When you finish, draw and color the three onto a poster.

Enrichment - internet
Find three Web sites that include information about bullfighting. List the addresses of each site and include a three-sentence summary of what you find at each site.

_____
_____
_____
_____
_____
_____
_____
_____

25 - El fútbol

Name: _____

Date: _____

Class: _____

Hechos Importantes
Read and say the following football terms out loud and in Spanish with your teacher.

What would a Sunday be without a good soccer game in a park or soccer stadium? Soccer is the most popular sport in the Spanish-speaking world. The Aztec stadium in Mexico City and the Bernabéu stadium in Madrid each seat more than 100,000 spectators. The Real Madrid team in Madrid, the Cruz Azul, and Chivas teams of Mexico, are among the most popular.

el balón - ball
la defensa - fullback
el delantero - forward
el entrenador - coach
el futbolista - soccer player
el equipo - team
el partido - game
el medio - halfback
la patada - kick
el tiro - shot
el portero - goalkeeper
el gol - goal
los aficionados - fans

Sopa de Letras
With a classmate, find and circle the following Spanish words.

```
Y Y V L A A O K J N N R U U F E H X T O
Q X W O F S I R H T U Y O V L A Z O T W
B T D S D N J W I U D J W E A B X T Z F
F Q D A N E G B R T C J N N P B K Z G I
T B B F B F C J B K L T G M A F U B Q I
A A B I G E T E F M R E L F T F W L V N
N B R C D D F K L E R L V K A G B B P I
L M W I H A J R N E X O O I D E M L E P
X L E O O L F A X D Q P V Q A I Y D W L
K T N N I R D S I K X U G X K I C I O N
Z J H A P O E Z W I Y Z I D B K Z D K W
P Q Y D R T L T R A H B P P J A I M P S
C F W O X Z O X N P Q O J H O T U U W H
N W I S E B S K L A A N A M R N T E P L
W F Z Z I W E P J H L S U A S X L Y X E
A T S I L O B T U F L E P G A B O U J H
K I T J Q H A F F N T L D C A U G J Z M
E L P O R T E R O Q E E P L P L L K M T
B N B G A Q H F P X O C Ó V E Q E F X J
H X J P V P L G P O C N Y Y S I F L H L
```

EL BALÓN
EL DELANTERO
EL ENTRENADOR
EL EQUIPO
EL FUTBOLISTA
EL GOL
EL MEDIO
EL PARTIDO
EL PORTERO
EL TIRO
LA DEFENSA
LA PATADA
LOS AFICIONADOS

A
ALSOP
74

25 - El fútbol

Conversación

With a classmate, read and say the following dialogue between two friends talking about an upcoming soccer game.

Alberto:	María, ¿vas al partido de Chivas y Cruz Azul?
María:	Sí, ¿vas? ¿Cuándo es?
Alberto:	Sí, voy. Es este domingo (*this Sunday*).
María:	¿Qué equipo (*team*) va a ganar?
Alberto:	Las Chivas, por supuesto(*of course*).
María:	Creo que no. Cruz Azul va a ganar.
Alberto:	¿Quieres ir (*do you want to go*) conmigo?
María:	Pues, claro que sí (*of course*).
Alberto:	El partido es en el Estadio Azteca.
María:	Pues, ¿a qué hora pasas por mí?
Alberto:	Este domingo, a las doce. Nos vemos.
María:	Gracias, Alberto. Te veo este domingo

note: Chivas team represents Guadalajara and Cruz Azul, Mexico City.

Teatro

Role play with a classmate a conversation between old friends about an upcoming soccer game. Act out in front of the class. Include vocabulary from the **Hechos Importantes** and **Conversación** sections.

_____

_____

_____

_____

_____

Work in pairs. Role play a conversation about soccer with your teacher. Include vocabulary from the **Hechos Importantes** and **Conversación** sections.

_____

_____

_____

_____

_____

25 - El fútbol

Name: _____

Date: _____

Class: _____

Juego
Write in the missing letters to complete the following Spanish soccer words.

1. p__r__i__o
2. e__u__p__
3. p__r__e__o
4. e__t__d__o
5. g__l
6. b__l__n
7. d__f__n__a
8. p__t__d__
9. m__d__o
10. t__r__

Proyecto
Work in groups of four. Videotape a commercial for an upcoming soccer match between the Chivas and Cruz Azul in Aztec Stadium in Mexico City! Write the script in the space below.

_____
_____
_____
_____
_____
_____
_____

Enrichment - internet
Find a Web site that includes information on either the Chivas of Guadalajara or Cruz Azul of Mexico City. List the Web site below and a summary of the information you find.

_____
_____
_____
_____
_____
_____
_____
_____

26 - La Navidad

Name: _____

Date: _____

Class: _____

Hechos Importantes
Let's practice some Christmas vocabulary.

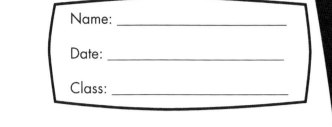

It's Christmas in Spain and Mexico. The Christmas markets in Madrid and Barcelona are aglow with ornaments and lights. Families go out in Mexico to sing at the Posadas, nine nights of visiting and singing. Children break piñatas! Los Reyes Magos will bring the children their gifts on January 6. ¡Feliz Navidad!

los nacimientos - crib scenes
el árbol navideño - Christmas tree
los Reyes Magos - the Three Kings
la Nochebuena - Christmas Eve
la Misa de Gallo - Midnight Mass
la Pastorela - medieval miracle plays
la bola de nieve - snow ball
el hombre de nieve - snow man
los villancicos - Christmas carols
la iglesia - church
los regalos - gifts
la vela - candle

Crucigrama
With a classmate, complete the following crossword puzzle.

Across
2. snow ball
6. Christmas carols
8. gifts
9. Christmas tree
10. snow man
11. candle

Down
1. Midnight Mass
3. church
4. crib scenes
5. Christmas Eve
6. Medieval miracle play
7. The Three Kings

ALSOP
77

26 - La Navidad

Name: _____

Date: _____

Class: _____

Conversación

With a classmate, read and say the following dialogue between two friends talking about Christmas.

Pancho: Inés, ¿quieres ir (*do you want to go*) a la Misa de Gallo?

Inés: Sí, ¿me invitas (*are you inviting me*)?

Pancho: Sí. Pero ahora (*now*) te invito al mercado para comprar unas figuras   para mi nacimiento.

Inés: ¿Hay (*Are there*) ornamentos para los árboles navideños?

Pancho: Sí. ¿Vas (*are you going*)?

Inés: ¿Cuándo vamos al mercado navideño?

Pancho: Ahorita (*right now*).

Inés: Pues, vámonos (*let's go*).

Pancho: Primero, te invito para un chocolate caliente.

Inés: Gracias, ¡qué muchacho eres!

Pancho: Por nada (*you're welcome*). Eres mi chica ideal.

Teatro

In a group of three, role play a conversation between you and your mother and father about Christmas in Spain and Mexico. Act out in front of the class. Include vocabulary from the **Hechos Importantes** and **Conversación** sections.

_____
_____
_____
_____
_____
_____

Work in pairs. Talk with your friend and invite him/her to a Christmas event in Mexico or Spain. Include vocabulary from the **Hechos Importantes** and **Conversación** sections.

_____
_____
_____
_____
_____
_____
_____

26 - La Navidad

Name: _____

Date: _____

Class: _____

Juego
With a classmate, unscramble these Spanish words and give their meaning in English.

1. remcaod
2. psodaa
3. lvilnaicoc
4. ed sMia lolaG al
5. boálr vaniedoñ
6. cimnaeiotn
7. al ocNehubnea
8. sol eyRse gMaso
9. agerlso
10. albo de ineev

_____
_____
_____
_____
_____
_____
_____
_____
_____
_____

Proyecto
Work in groups of three. In the space below practice drawing and labeling three greeting cards, one to your Spanish teacher, one to your best friend, and one to your favorite relative. When finished, put the drawings and words onto paper for use as a Christmas card!

Pistas-hints
Feliz Navidad, Felices Pascuas, Que Dios te bendiga, Que goces de estas navidades, Te deseo mucha alegría.

Enrichment - Dibujemos
In the space below draw *un(a) árbol navideño, un nacimiento, un mercado navideño, un hombre de nieve,* and *la Nochebuena.*

27 - El Día de los Muertos

Name: _____

Date: _____

Class: _____

Hechos Importantes

Día de los Muertos means **Day of the Dead**
and is celebrated in Mexico on November 1 and 2.
This is a special holiday when **families
(familias)** remember loved ones who have died.
Some special foods are **candy skulls (calaveras)**
and **bread of the dead (pan de los muertos)** that
is baked in the shape of a skull and crossbones. In
homes, families set out **pictures (fotos)**, **candles (velas)**,
flowers (flores), **incense (incienso)**, and **food (comida)**
on an **altar (altar)** where families bring out **favorite
items of the deceased person (ofrendas-offerings)**.
In the **evening (noche)**, families visit **cemeteries (panteones)**,
clean the graves, leave flowers and food, light candles,
and await the spirit of the **deceased loved one (muerto)**.

Sopa de Letras
With a classmate, find
and circle the
Spanish words
listed
below.

```
E F V G P L F I E Q A L R R V S A S H L
H S M J L J K L V K A U X A V Q A X O A
C G E L H H S I G S Q Y Y U T D K Z I S
O K N N C R L L V I Z R N B N L F Z R F
N V R K O G R E M J I J J E Y Z A J N O
A A Y H Q E L K Q V L X R W I P R L B T
L I A I L A T O R U Z F E S I N A W E O
Y N P L S A L N Y F O A D I M O C A L S
M A G I F R S X A S R M M S A A M I C W
V Z K R U C A F A P X X W A Y Z N O M T
B O V Y D P D L L B S D D I I I X C X I
V V F E E H R R L O M O L L Z M G A D M
E L I N C I E N S O R Q L I D P J R H L
W D D Q O O U E U V K E F M E B M S J P
W A S J L S M O R B J F S A A I Z O N R
K U F Q X H U Y J K R D M F Z D E A E X
T H D C V J L Y H J R X T S D U P K Z N
S A R E V A L A C S A L A A C L E J C B
D K R N B Q D X B Q J Q Q L E R D W O H
L X Y Z F F M J I L F G V Y D H F I N U
```

EL ALTAR
EL INCIENSO
EL PAN
LA COMIDA
LA NOCHE
LAS CALAVERAS
LAS FAMILIAS
LAS FLORES
LAS FOTOS
LAS OFRENDAS
LAS VELAS
LOS PANTEONES

A
ALSOP

80

www.teachersdiscovery.com

27 - El Día de los Muertos

Name: _____

Date: _____

Class: _____

Conversación
With a classmate, read and say the following
dialogue between Berta and Daniel.

Berta: Buenos días, Daniel.

Daniel: Hola, Berta. ¿Qué pasa (*What's happening*)?

Berta: Hoy es Día de los Muertos.

Daniel: Sí, voy a la tienda (*I'm going to the store*) para comprar (*buy*) calaveras.

Berta: ¡Qué bueno! Tenemos una ofrenda para mi abuelo (*grandpa*).

Daniel: Y tenemos una ofrenda para mi tía (*aunt*).

Berta: Por la noche, voy a pasar por el panteón.

Daniel: Sí, voy a limpiar (*clean*) la tumba(*grave*).

Berta: Mi familia va a poner (*put*) flores y velas.

Daniel: Bueno, voy a comer (*eat*) una comida especial.

Berta: Te veo más tarde (*I'll see you later*).

Daniel: Adiós.

Teatro

Role play with a classmate. Create a conversation with a friend describing what you each
will do to celebrate Día de los Muertos. Write a six-sentence conversation that takes place
between the two of you. Include vocabulary from the **Hechos Importantes** and
Conversación sections.

_____

_____

_____

_____

_____

_____

Work in pairs. Imagine you are an exchange student from Mexico. Create a conversation
explaining this holiday to your American host family. Include vocabulary from the **Hechos
Importantes** and **Conversación** sections.

_____

_____

_____

_____

A

ALSOP

27 - El Día de los Muertos

Name: _____

Date: _____

Class: _____

Juego

Unscramble the following words and give the English meaning.

1. leav _____
2. rafedno _____
3. acodim _____
4. avraelacs _____
5. coneh _____
6. ootf _____
7. tserumo _____
8. ferslo _____
9. npa _____
10. mafliia _____

Proyecto

In groups of three, prepare a diorama(using a shoe box)of an *ofrenda*. Choose a pet or famous personality as the theme of your *ofrenda*. Be sure to include candles, flowers, photo(s) of the person/pet, foods, beverages, and other decorations and items the person/pet enjoyed in his/her life.

Enrichment - internet

Search the Internet for more information on *Día de los Muertos*. What additional information could you find? Record it here. Did you find any new words? Be sure to include them with English meanings.

_____
_____
_____
_____
_____
_____

28 -La comida mexicana

Name: _____

Date: _____

Class: _____

Hechos Importantes

A typical Mexican **breakfast (el desayuno)** includes **bolillos** and some **huevos rancheros.** **Lunch (el almuerzo)** is the largest meal. Family members often get together to lunch at home. **Supper (la cena)** is usually a lighter meal. Practice the following Mexican food vocabulary out loud with your teacher.

el bolillo - bread roll
el melón - melon
las fresas - strawberries
el arroz - rice
el pollo - chicken
los chiles - hot peppers
las tortillas - tortillas
los tomates - tomatoes
la lechuga - lettuce
el queso - cheese
la carne de res - beef
los huevos - eggs
el flan - custard
los tacos al pastor - tacos made with seasoned pork cooked on a spit, sometimes served with pineapple
el helado - ice cream
la torta - cake
las enchiladas- tortillas, meat and sauce

Across
3. beans
4. strawberries
7. enchiladas
9. tortillas
10. ice cream
13. cake
14. eggs
15. custard
16. bread roll

Down
1. beef
2. chicken
3. chiles
4. tacos with pork
5. melon
6. lettuce
8. rice
11. tomatoes
12. cheese

Crucigrama
With a classmate, complete the following crossword puzzle.

28 - La comida mexicana

Name: _____

Date: _____

Class: _____

Conversación

With a classmate, read and say the following dialogue between two relatives talking about dinner (lunch).

Sofía:	Rodrigo, ¿qué hay para comer?
Rodrigo:	Hay tortillas, queso, sopa de elote (*corn*), arroz con pollo y flan.
Sofía:	Rodrigo, ¿vas a comer mucho?
Rodrigo:	Claro que sí (*of course*). Me gusta mucho comer.
Sofía:	Sí. Me gusta mucho el arroz con pollo.
Rodrigo:	Me gustan las tortillas con queso y el flan.
Sofía:	¿Y qué hay para beber (*drink*)?
Rodrigo:	Hay agua, leche, té o café.
Sofía:	Pues, vamos a sentarnos a la mesa (*at the table*).
Rodrigo:	Las damas (*ladies*) primero. Siéntate (*sit down*).
Sofía:	¡Buen provecho (*enjoy your meal*)!

Teatro

Work with a classmate. Hold a conversation about Mexican food. Act out in front of the class. Include vocabulary from the **Hechos Importantes** and **Conversación** sections.

_____

_____

_____

_____

_____

_____

Work in pairs. You are eating a Mexican meal at a Mexican friend's house. Include vocabulary from the **Hechos Importantes** and **Conversación** sections.

_____

_____

_____

_____

_____

28 - La comida mexicana

Name: _____

Date: _____

Class: _____

Juego
Work with a classmate to unscramble these
Spanish words and give their meaning in English.

1.   chienalsda   _____
2.   opllo   _____
3.   olbioll   _____
4.   rorza   _____
5.   srfesa   _____
6.   lehaod   _____
7.   ortitlals   _____
8.   aímz   _____
9.   lichse   _____
10.   ulecgha   _____

Proyecto
Work in pairs. Search the Internet and find a Mexican recipe. Present the recipe to class as if
you and your friend are TV cooks! Write the Web site address and the recipe in the space
below. Prepare the recipe at home, if you have time!

Enrichment - Dibujemos
In the space below, draw a dining table with four people seated at the table. Draw and label
a typical Mexican dinner (lunch).

29 - La comida española

Name: _____

Date: _____

Class: _____

Hechos Importantes
Let's travel to Madrid. We are in the **barrio** (neighborhood) of Salamanca. It is lunchtime. This is the biggest meal of the day. Let's check out the **plato del día** in the café. Since it is hot, and we are in the month of June, let's sit down at an outdoor café. Remember, Spaniards prepare many dishes in olive oil! Let's see what is on today's menu. Practice the pronunciation of the following words out loud with your teacher.

Crucigrama
With a classmate, complete the following crossword puzzle.

el gazpacho - cold tomato soup
el pan - bread
el cordero - lamb
la merluza - fish (hake)
la paella - rice and seafood dish
el flan - custard
la limonada - limonade
un refresco - refreshment

las patatas bravas - spicy potato wedges
los calamares - squid
los boquerones - anchovies
el pulpo - octopus
las aceitunas - olives
el chorizo - sausage
el queso manchego - cheese from la Mancha

Across
3. custard
5. squid
6. seafood and rice dish
7. anchovies
8. lamb

Down
1. bread
2. cold tomato soup
4. spicy potato wedges

29 - La comida española

Name: _____

Date: _____

Class: _____

Conversación

With a classmate, read and say the following dialogue between two tourists in Madrid. They are trying to decide where to eat.

Alfonso:	Nuria, ¿quieres (*do you want*) comer (*to eat*) en un café o en una tasca?
Nuria:	Quiero (*I want*) comer (*to eat*) en una tasca.
Alfonso:	Podemos (*we can*) comer en tres tascas diferentes.
Nuria:	Sí, quiero probar (*to try*) el queso manchego.
Alfonso:	En otra tasca podemos (*we can*) probar el pulpo.
Nuria:	Y en otra tasca quiero probar (*to try*) los boquerones.
Alfonso:	Pues me gusta (*I like*) esta idea.
Nuria:	Vale (*Okay*).
Alfonso:	Pues vamos a entrar.
Nuria:	Tengo mucha hambre (*I am very hungry*).
Alfonso:	Bien, vamos a comer (*let's eat*).

Teatro

Role play with a classmate that you are in Madrid with a friend. You decide where and what you want to eat. Act out in front of the class. Include vocabulary from the **Hechos Importantes** and **Conversación** sections.

_____

_____

_____

_____

_____

Work in pairs. Tell your mother or father about Spanish food. Include vocabulary from the **Hechos Importantes** and **Conversación** sections.

_____

_____

_____

_____

_____

_____

29 - La comida española

Name: _____

Date: _____

Class: _____

Juego
Write in the missing letters to complete the following Spanish food words.

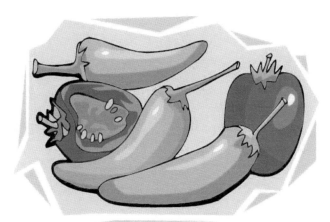

1. b__q__e__o__e__
2. __e__l__z__
3. __u__p__
4. a__e__t__n__s
5. p__t__t__s b__a__a__
6. f__a__
7. g__z__a__ __o
8. q__e__o
9. c__r__e__o
10. p__e__ __a
11. ch__r__z__

Proyecto
Work in groups of four. Videotape a commercial for an outdoor café in Madrid. Include some typical foods on your menu. Write the script in the space below.

Enrichment - internet
Do a search and find the recipe for a typical Spanish dish. List the Web site below and a summary of the information you find.

_____

_____

_____

_____

_____

_____

_____

30 - La música latina

Name: _____

Date: _____

Class: _____

Hechos Importantes

Can there be any music as rhythmic as Latin-American music? Here are some names of popular Latin music: **la salsa**, **el merengue**, **la cumbia**. There is **la música norteña, la música mariachi y rock**. Who are some of the popular Latin singers? Let's repeat some of their names!

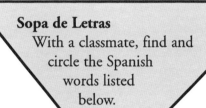

Shakira
Ricky Martin
Juan Luis Guerra
Celia Cruz
Alejandro Fernández
La India
Jerry Rivera
Gloria Estefan
Marc Anthony

Sopa de Letras
With a classmate, find and circle the Spanish words listed below.

```
A R I D T Y I J F J J M L U J L U G I G
K L E O T N U P M O U B F T K L L K J J
K E E H H O A Z S H A K I R A O V Q P J
W Z I J D H D R Z I N E B F R W I O B I
Z T J G A T C B E S L O I I U J F P P M
U R K D O N E R G V U V A V P D K U Y R
S H M S T A D X N P I E R A V Z B P D X
A X L T U C Y R D M S R S G I T P Z K C
N Z M B A R Z Q O T G K Y R G M F G M Z
T Z M L A A B D E F U B W R B B Y O U E
A J I U K M X F E A E O L B R Y H R Q T
N K I H S C A C V W R R N A H E C D J Y
A I C K L N L D L Z R A N C I A J Y X I
E X Q K K B R C G A A S P Á I N G V E Y
H S W A T D Y R J C E A R L N N D F E J
N I T R A M Y K C I R C E P C D Q I H J
W M R N T X I I H Q Q C E S R J E H A N
Y X F O U S A V K D D F Y N J W F Z F X
K K L Y O I S I F N C L H B I O M D N E
O I P T M Z Q L N E I H M E X C O L S F
```

ALEJANDRO
FERNÁNDEZ
CELIA CRUZ
GLORIA ESTEFAN
JERRY RIVERA
JUAN LUIS GUERRA
LA INDIA
MARC ANTHONY
RICKY MARTIN
SANTANA
SHAKIRA

30 - La música latina

Name: _____

Date: _____

Class: _____

Conversación

With a classmate, read and say the following dialogue between two students talking about an upcoming concert.

Celia:	Tomás, ¿vas al concierto de Shakira?
Tomás:	Sí, ¿vas tú?
Celia:	Sí, voy con una amiga.
Tomás:	Es este sábado. Empieza (*it begins*) a las nueve.
Celia:	¿Te gusta (*do you like*) la música de Shakira?
Tomás:	Sí, mucho. La música tiene mucho ritmo.
Celia:	Y la voz de Shakira es fabulosa.
Tomás:	Tengo todos sus CDs.
Celia:	Yo también.
Tomás:	Pues, te veo este sábado en el concierto. Adiós.
Celia:	Adiós, hasta el sábado.

Teatro

Role play with a classmate a conversation between a teacher and a student about Latin music. Act out in front of the class. Include vocabulary from the **Hechos Importantes** and

_____
_____
_____
_____
_____
_____
_____

Work in pairs. You tell your mother or father why you want to go to a Ricky Martin concert. Include vocabulary from the **Hechos Importantes** and **Conversación** sections.

_____
_____
_____
_____
_____
_____
_____
_____

A

ALSOP

90

30 - La música latina

Name: _____

Date: _____

Class: _____

Juego
Unscramble the names of these Latin singers.

1. narMit ycRik _____
2. akShria _____
3. fEtsena loGrai _____
4. aReivr erJry _____
5. zrCu leCai _____
6. aMcr thAnnoy _____
7. drAljeano nFeárnzed _____

Proyecto
Work in pairs. Search the Internet and find instructions for a Latin dance. Select either the *salsa*, *cumbia*, or *merengue*. Present the dance steps to the class as if you were a dance instructor. Write the Web site address and dance steps in the space below. Bring in a CD of Latin music to serve as the music for your dance lesson! For extra credit, sing some lines from one of the songs in Spanish!

_____
_____
_____
_____
_____
_____

Enrichment - Dibujemos
In the space below, draw a CD cover for a popular CD of one of the Latin singers mentioned in the **Hechos Importantes**. Label in Spanish.

31 - Los animales

Name: _____

Date: _____

Class: _____

Hechos Importantes
Madrid boasts a large city zoo with a wide variety of animals. Mexico City has its city zoo in Chapultepec Park. Both zoos have a panda. Practice the pronunciation of the following animal vocabulary words out loud with your teacher.

el tigre - tiger
el oso - bear
el caimán - alligator
el camello - camel
el mono - monkey
el pájaro - bird
el rinoceronte - rhino
el leopardo - leopard
el águila - eagle
la jirafa - giraffe

el león - lion
el oso panda - panda
la serpiente - snake
la cebra - zebra
el gorila - gorilla
el flamenco - flamingo
el hipopótamo - hippopotamus
la pantera - panther
el elefante - elephant
la foca - seal

Across
1. zebra
4. bear
6. camel
7. lion
10. gorilla
11. rhino
12. elephant

Down
2. monkey
3. panda bear
5. panther
6. tiger
8. giraffe
9. seal

Crucigrama
Working with a classmate, complete the following crossword puzzle.

31 - Los animales

Name: _____

Date: _____

Class: _____

Conversación

Working with a classmate, read and say the following dialogue between two visitors at the zoo in Madrid. They are trying to decide what animals to see.

Pablo:	Pilar, ¡qué zoológico tan bello (*what a pretty zoo*)!
Pilar:	Quiero ver (*I want to see*) los leones.
Pablo:	Quiero ver los gorilas.
Pilar:	Quiero ver los pájaros.
Pablo:	Quiero ver las serpientes.
Pilar:	Quiero ver los elefantes.
Pablo:	Tú, primero (*first*). Vamos a ver los leones.
Pilar:	Vale (*Okay*). Luego (*then*) podemos (*we can*) ver los gorilas.
Pablo:	Vale. Pasa (*Go ahead*).
Pilar:	Los leones están dormidos (*asleep*).
Pablo:	Mejor (*Better*). Vamos a ver los gorilas.

Teatro

Working with a classmate, role play that you are planning a visit to the zoo in Chapultepec Park, Mexico City. Mention what animals you want to see. Act out in front of the class. Include vocabulary from the **Hechos Importantes** and **Conversación** sections.

_____
_____
_____
_____
_____
_____

Work in pairs. Tell your Spanish teacher what animals are your favorites. Include vocabulary from the **Hechos Importantes** and **Conversación** sections.

_____
_____
_____
_____
_____

A
ALSOP

93

31 - Los animales

Name: _____

Date: _____

Class: _____

Juego
Write in the missing letters to complete the following Spanish words.

1. e__e__a__t__
2. __i__r__
3. c__i__á__
4. c__m__ll__
5. __o__i__a
6. __o__a
7. f__a__e__c__
8. __s__
9. l__o__a__d__
10. r__n__c__r__n__e

Proyecto
Work in groups of four. Videotape a commercial for a visit to the zoo in Chapultepec Park in Mexico City. Write the script in the space below.

Enrichment - internet
Do a search and find information about the zoo in Madrid, Spain. List the Web site below and a summary of the information you find. Include some of the animals. If you have no Internet access, use your library!

_____

_____

_____

_____

_____

_____

32 - Los pintores

Name: _____

Date: _____

Class: _____

Hechos Importantes
Spain has had its share of great painters. Let's repeat their names!

Diego Velázquez
Francisco de Goya
Pablo Picasso
Salvador Dalí

Mexico has also had its share of great painters. Let's repeat!
Diego Rivera
Frida Kahlo
Rufino Tamayo.

```
L T S N R P W J M D O N P L F R F Q F G
F C I I S U L S C V T T T R F Z F Z Q N
J R I K B O T K K M H K A Í Y M U O V I
D B I U Z M J G V T I N E L Y S R X Y T
W N P D L C B F Z P C Q X A C Y T G C C
O G F D A G A H Y I E L T D N Q Q O G I
H S Z G Q K M Y S Y G C O R G V H B J R
J E S F U M A C A J M Y G O F J C P S M
A H T A N W O H B O A Y H D X S I R Q P
Z D K A C D T A L M B D J A M E V P C P
Z B E H E I H A A O Y J E V N G E Y X F
Z I I G N U P T D Q O B G L P D J S G D
P J O N W X O O J F C P G A Y X M D U E
K Y C S B N Z A L P B N H S H O L I B X
A S U E I H P J X B B T S M K L T S E Y
W L X F O Z L C L E A T Z X A U C X D H
O Y U R W K Y M L Z N P D N X P N T E B
M R Z K W U D I E G O R I V E R A G M G
F H H G I C X M S W V D K B S H T X Z J
Z Y Z E U Q Z Á L E V O G E I D B Z Y Y
```

Sopa de Letras
With a classmate, find and circle the following Spanish and Mexican painters.

DIEGO RIVERA
DIEGO VELÁZQUEZ
FRANCISCO DE GOYA
FRIDA KAHLO
PABLO PICASSO
RUFINO TAMAYO
SALVADOR DALÍ

ALSOP

95

32 - Los pintores

Name: _____

Date: _____

Class: _____

Conversación

With a classmate, read and say out loud the following dialogue between two art students talking about Spanish and Mexican painters.

Patricia: Enrique, ¿te gustan las pinturas (*do you like the paintings*) de Velázquez y Goya?

Enrique: Sí, pero me gustan más las pinturas de Diego Rivera.

Patricia: Pues, me gustan más las pinturas de Salvador Dalí.

Enrique: También me gustan las pinturas de Picasso.

Patricia: La verdad es que me gustan más las pinturas de Frida Kahlo.

Enrique: Sí, ¡qué mujer (*what a woman*)!

Patricia: Mañana vamos a ir al museo (*museum*) para ver (*to see*) unas pinturas.

Enrique: Claro que sí (*of course*).

Patricia: Te veo a la una (*I'll see you at l:00*).

Enrique: Bien, nos vemos a la una. Adiós. Hasta pronto.

Patricia: Adiós, hasta mañana

Teatro

Working with a classmate, role play a conversation between a student and teacher about Spanish and Mexican art. Act out in front of the class. Include vocabulary from the **Hechos Importantes** and **Conversación** sections.

_____
_____
_____
_____
_____
_____

Work in pairs. You tell your friend why you want to go to the art museum. Include vocabulary from the **Hechos Importantes** and **Conversación** sections.

_____
_____
_____
_____
_____

A
ALSOP

96

32 - Los pintores

Name: _____

Date: _____

Class: _____

Juego
Unscramble the names of the following famous Mexican and Spanish painters.

1. ciPaoss aPbol   _____
2. alDí alSvardo   _____
3. oGya aFrnicsoc ed   _____
4. eRivar eiDgo   _____
5. aKlho aFird   _____
6. onRfui amTaoy   _____
7. elVázuqez eiDgo   _____

Proyecto
Work in pairs. Do a report on the life of one of the painters mentioned in **Hechos Importantes.** Use your library or the Internet. Present your report to the class in the form of a TV broadcast. Use props when possible!

_____
_____
_____
_____
_____
_____
_____

Enrichment - Dibujemos
Do a search on the Internet, visit your library, or use a picture from your textbook. Find a painting by one of the painters mentioned in **Hechos Importantes**. Draw and color your version of the painting. Give the title in Spanish. Practice in the space below.

33 - Los escritores

Name: _____

Date: _____

Class: _____

Hechos Importantes

Let's repeat the names of some of Spain's great writers! **Miguel de Cervantes**, **Lope de Vega**, **Gustavo Bécquer**, and **Federico García Lorca.** Let's try some of the great Mexican writers! **Sor Juana de la Cruz, Octavio Paz, Carlos Fuentes. Cervantes** was a great **novelista** (novelist). He wrote the famous novel, **EL QUIJOTE. Lope de Vega** was a great **dramaturgo** (playwright). **Bécquer** and **Lorca** were great **poetas** (poets). **Sor Juana** and **Octavio Paz** were poets. **Carlos Fuentes** wrote novels and essays.

Sopa de Letras
With a classmate, find and circle the names of Spanish and Mexican writers listed below.

```
B G B I H R L M V H K S E N E G S A I W
P P U Q D T Q H Z V V R B G Z E J C B D
U U J S V G Y N X U K I F V T P B R I S
I V F T T P J Z M L L X F N I K M O F L
Z H S S H A J S O C E S A R G O I L Z J
T S I C I P V P W D G V V H Q Y S A C Z
W I J A I H E O Q I R O Q Y S T D Í H E
W R K W C D B H B E O E S T Z M C C E O
Z M M D E I R Q C É L B O Y F H A R T W
C V S V R R F E K D C Z I G L X R A P O
H K E E V O D H T V W Q Z A E O L G U F
A G X E Y L J P M H T I U T D M O O X Z
A P R K E J E A N B N H I E Y V S C M K
Y P E U S G G V H B G S Y K R P F I W C
I E G L Z H R A F T S P M E D N U R J A
P I R Q E I C T S G U M R L N V E E E K
M Z A P O I V A T C O H K X H W N D Q R
O H S L Q G J F K B D R W G V S T E M N
S O R J U A N A D E L A C R U Z E F G J
G K B U O V B Z R P Q C E Y K M S Z U H
```

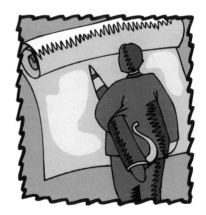

CARLOS FUENTES
FEDERICO GARCÍA LORCA
GUSTAVO BÉCQUER
LOPE DE VEGA
MIGUEL DE CERVANTES
OCTAVIO PAZ
SOR JUANA DE LA CRUZ

A
ALSOP

98

33 - Los escritores

Conversación

With a classmate, read and say the following dialogue between two Spanish teachers at your high school. They are trying to decide which writers to study.

Héctor: Marisol, este semestre quiero enseñar (*I want to teach*) a Cervantes.

Marisol: Quiero enseñar (*I want to teach*) a García Lorca.

Héctor: Me gusta (*I like*) más (*more*) Cervantes.

Marisol: Me gusta mucho Sor Juana de la Cruz.

Héctor: Me gusta más Octavio Paz.

Marisol: Pues, ¿qué vamos a hacer (*what are we going to do?*).

Héctor: Vamos a enseñar a Lope de Vega.

Marisol: Bueno (*okay*), está bien.

Héctor: Decididos (*decided*).

Marisol: Vamos a tomar un café (*Let's drink a coffee*).

Héctor: Bueno, siéntate (*sit down*).

Teatro

Working with a classmate, role play a conversation about great writers. Include writers from the **Hechos Importantes** section.

_____
_____
_____
_____
_____
_____
_____

Work in pairs. Role play that one of you is a Spanish teacher and the other is a student who tells him/her about his/her favorite writers. Use information from the **Hechos Importantes** section.

_____
_____
_____
_____
_____
_____
_____

33 - Los escritores

Name: _____

Date: _____

Class: _____

Juego
Write in the missing letters to complete the names of the following Mexican and Spanish writers.

1. M__g__e__ de C__r__a__t__s
2. F__d__r__c__ G__r__í__ L__r__a
3. L__p__ de V__g__
4. G__s__a__o B__c__u__r
5. C__r__o__ F__e__t__s
6. S__r J__a__a de l__ C__u__
7. O__t__v__o P__z

Proyecto
Work in a group of four. Make up a song about one of the writers from **Hechos Importantes.** Use information from the above section to help. Make the song match the melody of a popular song - new or old.

Enrichment - internet
Do a search on the Internet or visit your library. Find information about one of the writers in **Hechos Importantes.** List a summary of the information you find. Use the information and write an article about the writer for your school newspaper.

_____
_____
_____
_____
_____
_____
_____

1. El alfabeto - Pg. 1
Across
1. ve
4. ele
5. i griega
8. efe
11. eme
Down
2. eñe
3. zeta
5. i
7. ene
9. ese
10. te

Juego 1 - Pg. 3
1. español - Spanish
2. clase - class
3. mapa - map
4. música - music
5. banda - band
6. aire - air
7. señor - mister, sir
8. favorito - favorite
9. zona - zone
10. clásica - classic

2. Los saludos - Pg. 4
Across
3. me llamo
6. bien
8. buenas noches
9. buenos
10. hola
Down
1. por favor
2. adiós
4. buenos días
5. gracias
7. mucho gusto

Juego 2 - Pg. 6
1. hola - hello
2. buenos días - good morning
3. adiós - goodbye
4. hasta luego - see you later
5. buenas tardes - good afternoon
6. buenas noches - good night
7. bien - fine
8. así así - so-so
9. por favor - please
10. gracias - thanks

Los números 3 - Pg. 7

```
+ E + + E D I E C I O C H O Q S + + S +
+ + C V + + + + T + + + U + E + I + +
+ + E N + + + + + E + + I + + I É C + +
+ U + + O + + T + + I N + + + S + U + +
N + + + + + + R + C S + + I + + A + +
E T N I E V + + + E + + I C + + + T + +
+ + + + C + + + + + S + E C + + + R + +
+ + + + O + + + + + + I + + E + + O + +
C + + + D + + + + D + + + + I + + + +
+ A Z E I D + + + + + D O S + D + + +
+ + T + + + + + + + + + + + + + + E +
+ + + O + + O + + + + + + + + + + V +
+ + + + R C + + + + + + + + + + + E +
+ + + O H C + + + + + + + + + + + U E
+ + N O + + E + + + + + + + + + + N T
O U + + + + + + + + + + + + + + I E
+ C + + + + + + + + + + + + + + C I
+ + N + + + + + + + + + + + + + E S
+ + + I + + + + + + + + + + + + I +
+ T R E C E + + + + + + + + + + D +
```

(Over,Down,Direction)
CATORCE(1,9,SE)
CINCO(5,20,NW)
CUATRO(18,3,S)
DIECINUEVE(19,20,N)
DIECIOCHO(6,1,E)
DIECISIETE(17,10,NW)
DIECISÉIS(11,9,NE)
DIEZ(6,10,W)
DOCE(5,9,N)
DOS(13,10,E)
NUEVE(1,5,NE)
OCHO(7,12,SW)
ONCE(5,4,NW)
QUINCE(15,1,SW)
SEIS(16,1,S)
SIETE(20,18,N)
TRECE(2,20,E)
TRES(8,4,SE)
UNO(2,16,NE)
VEINTE(6,6,W)

Juego 3 - Pg. 9
1. siete
2. trece
3. nueve
4. diecinueve
5. veinte
6. once
7. ocho
8. cuatro
9. uno
10. seis

A
ALSOP
101

4. La hora del día - Pg. 10
Across
6. Son las cinco y diez
Down
1. de la mañana
2. Son las ocho menos diez.
3. Es la una
4. de la tarde
6. Es medianoche.

Juego 4 - Pg. 12
1. hora - time(hour)
2. media - half
3. once - eleven
4. cuarto - quarter
5. medianoche - midnight
6. tarde - afternoon
7. menos - minus
8. mañana - morning
9. qué - what
10. una - one

La ropa 5 - Pg. 13

```
L + + + + + + + L + L + + + + + + L +
O O + + + + + + A + O + + + + + + A +
S + S + + + B A S I M A C A L + + C +
C A + P + + U + V + + + + + + + O +
A + T + A F + A + A + + + + + + R +
L + + E A N Q + T + + + + + + B +
C + + N U U T E + + + + + N + + A +
E + D + E Q S A O R E R B M O S L E T +
T A E R + I A + L + + + + + R + + A +
I + O L M + + H + O + + + U + + + +
N S + A V + + + C + N + + + T + + + +
E + C + + E + + O A + E + + N + + + E
S A + + + + S + + G L + S + I + + J +
L O S G U A N T E S I + + C + + A + A
+ L A B L U S A I + + R + + L + R + + R
+ + + + + + + + D + + B + E T + + + R
+ + + + + + + + + O + + A L + + + O
+ + + + + + + + + + + E L + + + G
+ + + + + + + + + + + + + E + + + A
+ + + + + + + + + + + + + + + + + L
```

(Over,Down,Direction)
EL ABRIGO(16,19,NW)
EL CINTURÓN(15,16,N)
EL SOMBRERO(18,8,W)
EL TRAJE(14,18,NE)
EL VESTIDO(3,9,SE)
LA BLUSA(2,15,E)
LA BUFANDA(10,1,SW)
LA CAMISA(16,3,W)
LA CAMISETA(1,14,NE)
LA CHAQUETA(11,13,NW)
LA CORBATA(19,1,S)
LA GORRA(20,20,N)
LOS CALCETINES(1,1,S)
LOS GUANTES(1,14,E)
LOS PANTALONES(1,1,SE)
LOS VAQUEROS(12,1,SW)

Juego 5 - Pg. 15
1. falda - skirt
2. guantes - gloves
3. corbata - tie
4. vestido - dress
5. camisa - shirt
8. sombrero - hat
9. sudadera - sweat shirt
10. blusa - blouse

6. Los colores - Pg. 16
Across
1. turquesa
4. gris
8. anaranjado
9. violeta
11. negro
Down
2. amarillo
3. marrón
5. rosado
6. blanco
7. verde
10. azul

Juego 6 - Pg. 18
1. rojo - red
2. negro - black
3. verde - green
4. anaranjado - orange
5. blanco - white
6. marrón - brown
7. rosado - pink
8. azul - blue
9. gris - gray
10. amarillo - yellow

ALSOP
102

El tiempo 7 - Pg. 19

```
+ + + + + + + H + + + + + + O + + +
E + + + + + A A + H + + + D H + + +
+ C + + + C + C + + A + + A A + + + +
+ + A + + E + + E + + + C L C + + + +
+ + + H F + + + B + + + B E + + + + +
+ + + R O + + + U + + U M H F + + + +
+ + Í + + P + + E + N A + A + R + + + +
+ O + + + M + N Á L + + C O + E + + +
+ + + + + + + E T T + + + E D + + S + +
+ + + + + + + S I + + + C N + + + C +
+ + + + + + E E E T + + A A + + + + O
+ + + + + M + M + É + + L V + + + + +
+ + + + + P + + P + + U + O E + + + +
+ + + O + + + O + + + Q R N + + + +
H A C E V I E N T O + + + + Á + + + +
L O S E C A H + + + + + + T + + + +
O D N E I V O L L Á T S E + S + + + +
+ + + + + + + + + + + + + + E + + + +
+ + + + + + + + + + + + + + + + + + +
+ + + + + + + + + + + + + + + + + + +
```

(Over,Down,Direction)
ESTÁ LLOVIENDO(13,17,W)
ESTÁ NEVANDO(15,18,N)
ESTÁ NUBLADO(7,11,NE)
HACE BUEN TIEMPO(9,1,S)
HACE CALOR(14,6,S)
HACE FRESCO(11,2,SE)
HACE FRÍO(9,1,SW)
HACE MAL TIEMPO(17,2,SW)
HACE SOL(7,16,W)
HACE VIENTO(1,15,E)
QUÉ TIEMPO HACE(13,14,NW)

Juego 7 - Pg. 21
1. viento - windy
2. fresco - cool
3. sol - sunny
4. nevando - snowing
5. calor - warm
6. tiempo - weather
7. nublado - cloudy
8. mal - bad
9. lloviendo - raining
10. hace - it is

8. Los objetos de clase - Pg. 22
Across
4. la carpeta
6. el papel
7. el lápiz
8. el diccionario
9. el cuaderno
Down
1. el libro
2. la mochila
3. la regla
4. la calculadora
5. el bolígrafo

Juego 8 - Pg. 24
1. lápiz - pencil
2. regla - ruler
3. cuaderno - notebook
4. mochila - backpack
5. carpeta - folder
6. libro - book
7. calculadora - calculator
8. diccionario - dictionary
9. papel - paper
10. bolígrafo - pen

El verbo gustar 9 - Pg. 25

```
E + + + + + + + + + + + + + + + + M
T M + + + + + + + + + + + + + + + E
R + E + + + + + S + + + + + S + + G
A + + G + + + + E + + + + E + + + U
L + + + U + + + S + + + T S + + + S
E + + + + S + + + A + + E A + + + + T
A + + + + T + + L + G L + + + + + + A
T + + + + + A + C U C + + + + + + L
S + + + + + + L S S + + + + + + + A
U + + M E G U S T A E L E S P A Ñ O L M
G + + + + + A L L C + + + + + + Ú
E + + + + L N + N + I + + + + + S
T + + + A A + + A + + E + + + + I
+ + + C T + + + T + + N + + + + C
+ + + L S + + + S + + + C + + + A
+ + A U + + + + U + + + + I + + +
+ S G + + + + + G + + + + A + +
E E + + E T R A L E A T S U G E M + + +
T + + + + + + M + + + + + + + + +
+ + + + + + + + + + + + + + + + +
```

(Over,Down,Direction)
ME GUSTA EL ARTE(17,18,W)
ME GUSTA EL ESPAÑOL(4,10,E)
ME GUSTA LA CIENCIA(2,2,SE)
ME GUSTA LA MÚSICA(20,1,S)
ME GUSTAN LAS CLASES(10,19,N)
TE GUSTA EL ARTE(1,13,N)
TE GUSTA LA CLASE(14,5,SW)
TE GUSTAN LAS CLASES(1,19,NE)

Juego 9 - Pg. 27

1. inglés - English
2. ciencia - science
3. gustan - like
4. música - music
5. clase - class
6. español - Spanish
7. arte - art
8. computación - computer class
9. matemáticas - math
10. qué - what

Juego 10 - Pg. 30

1. quién - who
2. por qué - why
3. cuándo – when
4. dónde - where
5. cómo - how

La familia 11 - Pg. 31

```
+ + + + + + + E + + + + E L E L + + + +
A S O P S E A L L + + L + A L + A + + +
+ + + D + + + R + P E + + M A + + T + +
+ + + + A + + + E S A + + A B + + + Í +
+ + + + + Ñ + + P U + D + D U + + + + A
+ + O + + + U O + + N + R R E + + + + +
+ + J + + + S C + + + A + E L + + + + +
+ + I + + + O + + L + + L + O + + + + +
+ + H + + + + + + E A M I R P A L + + +
+ + L + + + + + + + + + + + + + + + + +
+ + E + + + + + + + + + + + + + + + + +
E + + + + A + + + + + + A + + + + + + +
+ L + + + L + + + + + D + E + + + + + +
+ + H L A H E R M A N A + L + + + + + +
+ + + E + + U + + + Ñ + Y + + A + + + +
+ + + + R + B + + U + E + + J + + + + +
E L T Í O M A + C + R + + I + + + + + +
+ + + + + + A A + N + + H + + + + + + +
+ + + + + + L N O + + A + + + + + + + +
+ + + + + + + O E L P R I M O + + + + +
```

(Over,Down,Direction)
EL ABUELO(15,1,S)
EL CUÑADO(10,9,NW)
EL ESPOSO(13,1,SW)
EL HERMANO(1,12,SE)
EL HIJO(3,11,N)
EL PADRE(8,1,SE)
EL PRIMO(10,20,E)
EL TÍO(1,17,E)
EL YERNO(15,13,SW)
LA ABUELA(7,19,N)
LA CUÑADA(7,19,NE)
LA ESPOSA(8,2,W)
LA HERMANA(4,14,E)
LA HIJA(11,20,NE)
LA MADRE(14,1,S)
LA NUERA(13,8,NW)
LA PRIMA(17,9,W)
LA TÍA(16,1,SE)

Juego 11 - Pg. 33

1. yerno
2. tío
3. prima
4. hermana
5. hija
6. madre
7. esposo
8. cuñado
9. hermano
10. abuela

12. El cuerpo - Pg. 34

Across

2. el ojo
4. la rodilla
5. la nariz
6. los dedos
8. el pie
9. la pierna
10. la boca

Down

1. el brazo
3. la cabeza
5. la oreja
6. la mano
7. el estómago

Juego 12 - Pg. 36

1. brazo - arm
2. oreja - ear
3. boca - mouth
4. rodilla - knee
5. cabeza - head
6. dedos - fingers
7. nariz - nose
8. pierna - leg
9. estómago - stomach
10. mano - hand

Los cuartos 13 - Pg. 37

```
+ + E + R + + + + + A + + + + + + + +
+ + + L + O + + + B + + + + + + E + +
+ + + + C + D + + O + + + + + + L + +
O + + + + U + E C A L A S A L + + C + +
N + + + + + A L M E L G A R A J E U L +
A + + + + + A R + O + A L + + + A + +
T + + E + A + + T + C A S + + + C R + +
Ó + + L L + + + + O S L + A + O + T + +
S + + D + + + + + A + + E + C + + O + +
L + + E + + + + L + + + + I + A + D + +
E + + S + + + A + + + + N + + + L E + +
+ + + V + + D + + + + A + + + + + B + +
+ + + Á + E + + + + + + + + + + A + +
+ + + N E + + + + + + + + + + + Ñ + +
+ + + S + + + + + + + + + + + + O + +
+ + T + + + + + + + + + + + + + + + +
+ A + + + + + + + + + + + + + + + + +
R + + + + + + + + + + + + + + + + + +
+ + + + + + + + + A S N E P S E D A L +
+ + + + + + + + + + + + + + + + + + +
```

(Over,Down,Direction)
EL COMEDOR(13,9,NW)
EL CUARTO(3,1,SE)
EL CUARTO DE BAÑO(18,2,S)
EL DESVÁN(4,7,S)
EL GARAJE(10,5,E)
EL SÓTANO(1,11,N)
LA ALCOBA(5,8,NE)
LA CASA(17,11,NW)
LA COCINA(19,5,SW)
LA DESPENSA(19,19,W)
LA SALA(15,4,W)
LA SALA DE ESTAR(13,6,SW)

Juego 13 - Pg. 39

1. alcoba
2. cuarto de baño
3. sala
4. comedor
5. cocina
6. sótano
7. desván
8. garaje
9. sala de estar
10. cuarto

14. La hora del día - Pg. 40

Across

4. sábado
8. agosto
9. domingo
11. junio
12. enero
13. abril
14. jueves
16. diciembre
17. octubre
18. viernes

Down

1. martes
2. febrero
3. miércoles
5. lunes
6. marzo
7. noviembre
10. mayo
14. julio
15. septiembre

Juego 14 - Pg. 42

1. agosto - August
2. sábado - Saturday
3. marzo - March
4. martes - Tuesda
5. domingo - Sunday
6. febrero - February
7. jueves - Thursday
8. octubre - October
9. miércoles - Wednesday
10. diciembre - December

El verbo ser 15 - Pg. 43

```
E + A + + + + + + + + + + + + E + E + +
+ R + N E S E S P A Ñ O L A R + S + A +
O + E + A + + + + + + + + E + I A + P +
+ C + S + I + + + + + S + N T + E A +
+ + I + I + B + + + G + T L + + S U +
+ + + D + N + M + + U + E A + E + D G +
+ + + + É + T + O A + L S + + S + E S A
+ + + + M + E P L I E + + + D + C E R
+ + + + + S O L G O A + + + E + H + O
+ + + + E + E N I T C + + + C + I + S
+ + + + + R T + S G + S + + O + L + E
+ + + + + E E I + + E + E + S + E + F
E T N A I D U T S E S E N + + T + + + O
+ + + + + + N + + B + + + T + A + + + R
+ + + + E + + + + O + + E R + + + P
+ + + + D + + + + + N + + + I + + + S
+ + + S A N A B U C S E I + + C + + + E
+ + E + + + + + + + + + + T + A + + + +
+ + + + + + + + + + + + + + A + + + + +
+ + + + + + + + + + + + + + + + + + + +
```

(Over,Down,Direction)

ERES BONITA(6,10,SE)
ERES GUAPO(16,1,SW)
ERES INTELIGENTE(1,1,SE)
ES ALTA(12,8,NE)
ES COLOMBIANA(14,12,NW)
ES CUBANA(12,17,W)
ES DE CHILE(18,4,S)
ES DE COSTA RICA(16,6,S)
ES DENTISTA(3,18,NE)
ES ESPAÑOLA(5,2,E)
ES ESTUDIANTE(12,13,W)
ES GUAPA(19,8,N)
ES INTELIGNTE(18,1,SW)
ES MÉDICO(8,10,NW)
ES PROFESORA(20,17,N)

Juego 15 - Pg. 45

1. eres
2. es
3. soy
4. guapo
5. alta
6. bonita
7. inteligente
8. español
9. cubano
10. médica

16. El verbo estar - Pg. 46

Across

1. Está contento

Down

1. ¿Cómo estás?
2. Estás enfermo.
3. Estoy bien.
4. Estoy cansado
5. Está en México.
6. Está triste.

Juego 16 - Pg. 48

1. estás
2. estoy
3. está
4. cómo
5. en
6. España
7. México
8. cansado
9. triste
10. enfermo

El verbo tener 17 - Pg. 49

```
+ + + + A + + + + + + + + T + A + + + +
+ + + + + R + + + + + + I + + L + + + +
+ + + + + + E + + + + E + + + I + + + +
+ + + + + + D + + N + + + + H + + + + +
+ + + + + + + N E + + + + + C + + + +
+ + + E + + S + N A + + + + + O + + + +
+ + + + N O + + + + B + + + + M + + + +
+ + + M E + + + + + A + + A + + + +
+ + + E + + I + + + J L + + L + + + +
+ + N + + + + T + + + E + + + + + + +
+ E + + + + O I R O T I R C S E L E + +
T + + + + + + + + + + V + + + + + + + +
+ + + + + + + + + + + + + + + + + + + +
T L + + + + + + + + + + + + + + + + + +
I + A + + + + + + + + + + + + + + + + +
E + + S + + + + + + + + + + + + + + + +
N + + + I + + + + + + + + + + + + + + +
E + + + L O G N E T + + E L D R A M A
S + + + + + L + + + + + + + + + + + + +
+ + + + + + + A + + + + + + + + + + + +
```

(Over,Down,Direction)
EL DRAMA(14,18,E)
EL ESCRITORIO(18,11,W)
LA BANDERA(13,9,NW)
LA MOCHILA(16,9,N)
LA SILLA(2,14,SE)
TENEMOS(1,12,NE)
TENGO(11,18,W)
TIENE(8,10,NW)
TIENEN(14,1,SW)
TIENES(1,14,S)
VIEJA(12,12,N)

Juego 17 - Pg. 51

1. drama-drama
2. tiene-he has
3. silla-chair
4. tengo-I have
5. bandera-flag
6. vieja-old
7. escritorio-desk
8. tenemos-we have
9. mochila-bookbag
10. tienes-you have

18. El verbo ir - Pg. 52

Across

5. ¿Quién va a Puerto Rico?

Down

1. Mi amigo(a) va a Puerto Rico.
2. ¿Adónde vas?
3. Voy a Nueva York.
4. Voy a Sevilla.
6. ¿Vas a casa?

Juego 18 - Pg. 54

1. dónde
2. vas
3. voy
4. quién
5. Barcelona
6. Puerto Rico
7. México
8. Sevilla

La comida 19 - Pg. 55

```
E L + + + + + L + L + E + + + + + E
+ L A + + + + A + A + R + + + + L +
+ + P L + + + F + S + T + + + P + +
+ + + E E + + R + P + S + + + O + O +
+ + A + R C + + U + A + O + + L + D + +
+ + + D + R H + T + P + P + L + A + + +
+ + + + A + O E A + A + L O + L + + + L
+ + + + + L + C + + S + E + E + + + A +
+ + + + + + A + A + F + + H + + + H + +
+ + + + + + + S + L R + L + + A + + +
+ + + + + + + + N + I E + + + M + + + +
+ + + + + + + + + E T E + + B + + + +
S E R B M U G E L S A L N U N + + + +
+ + + + + + + + + S L R T + A + + + +
+ + + + + + + + + + G + + E + P + + +
+ + + + + + + + + + U + + + + + L + +
+ + + + + + + + + E + + + + + + + E +
+ + + + + + + + S + L A C A R N E + +
+ + + + + É F A C L E + + + + + + +
+ + + + + + + + + + + + + + + + + + +
```

(Over,Down,Direction)
EL CAFÉ(11,19,W)
EL HELADO(12,11,NE)
EL PAN(19,17,NW)
EL PERRO CALIENTE(1,1,SE)
EL POLLO(20,1,SW)
EL POSTRE(13,8,N)
LA CARNE(11,18,E)
LA ENSALADA(12,14,NW)
LA FRUTA(9,1,S)
LA HAMBURGUESA(20,7,SW)
LA LECHE(2,1,SE)
LAS LEGUMBRES(12,13,W)
LAS PAPAS FRITAS(11,1,S)

Juego 19 - Pg. 57

1. postre-dessert
2. leche-milk
3. ensalada-salad
4. carne-meat
5. fruta-fruit
6. legumbres-vegetables
7. papas fritas-French fries
8. café-coffee
9. perro caliente-hot dog
10. hamburguesa-hamburger

20. Los sustantivos / adjetivos - Pg. 58

Across
3. El chico es guapo.
5. Los chicos son guapos.
7. José es alto.

Down
1. La chica es bonita.
2. Las chicas son bontias.
4. María es alta.
6. Los chicos son altos.

Juego 20 - Pg. 60

1. casas
2. las
3. son
4. bonitas
5. el
6. es
7. chico
8. guapo
9. altos (o altas)

La geografía 21 - Pg. 62

```
B + + A L E U Z E N E V + + Ú A + N O +
+ U + C O L O M B I A + + + Ñ R Ó + G +
+ + E + + + + + C + + Y A + I E + A +
+ + + N + + + + A + + P A C + + P I +
+ + + + O + + + + R + S + N U + + A T +
+ + + + E S + + + A E + U + + G R + N +
+ + + + C + A + + G Á S + + + G A + A +
+ + + + U + + I + U A T + + E + + R S +
C + + + A + + R A + + O N + + + B A +
+ A + + D + + + + E + + T G + + O + + P
+ + R + O + + + + + S I + + O L + C + +
+ + + A R + A U G A N A M + I B + H + +
Q + + + C + + S + A + + + V M É X I C O
+ U + + + A U + + + + + I + + + + L + +
+ + I + + C S D + + + A + + + + + E + +
+ + + T R A M I L + + + + + + + + + +
+ + + E O + + R + + + + + + + + + + +
+ + + + + + + D + + + + + + + + + + +
+ + + + + + + A + + + + + + + + + + +
+ + + + + + + M + + + + + + + + + + +
```

(Over,Down,Direction)
ARGENTINA(18,5,SW)
ASUNCIÓN(11,8,NE)
BOGOTÁ(16,12,NW)
BOLIVIA(18,9,SW)
BUENOS AIRES(1,1,SE)
CARACAS(1,9,SE)
CHILE(18,11,S)
COLOMBIA(4,2,E)
ECUADOR(5,6,S)
ESPAÑA(11,6,NE)
LIMA(9,16,W)
MADRID(8,20,N)
MANAGUA(13,12,W)
MÉXICO(15,13,E)
NICARAGUA(10,1,S)
PARAGUAY(20,10,NW)
PERÚ(18,4,NW)
QUITO(1,13,SE)
SANTIAGO(19,8,N)
SUCRE(8,13,SW)
VENEZUELA(12,1,W)

Juego 21 - Pg. 64

1. Bogotá, Colombia
2. Managua, Nicaragua
3. Buenos Aires, Aregentina
4. Madrid, España
5. Caracas, Venezuela
6. San Juan, Puerto Rico
7. La Ciudad de México
8. Sucre, Bolivia
9. Quito, Ecuador
10. Santiago, Chile

22. Tú-usted - Pg. 65

Across

2. ¿Estudias el español?
5. ¿Cómo estás?
6. ¿Adónde vas?
7. ¿Dónde vive usted?

Down

1. ¿Estudia usted el español?
3. ¿Adónde va usted?
4. ¿Dónde vives?

Juego 22 - Pg. 67

1. estás
2. está
3. tú
4. usted
5. vas
6. vive
7. vives
8. dónde
9. estudias
10. va

Los abrazos y los besos 23 - Pg. 68

```
+ + + + + + + + + S O + + + + + +
+ + + + + + + + + O + Z + + + + +
+ + + + S + + + Z + + A + + + + +
+ + + + + O + + A + + R + + + + +
+ + + + + Z R + + + B + + + + + +
+ + + + + B A + + + A + + + + + +
O Z A R B A E T R E U F N U + + + + +
+ + + + + + + + + B + U + + + + +
+ + + + + + + + + A + + + + + + +
+ + + + + + + + + + Y + + + + + +
+ + + + + + + + + + + S + + + + +
+ + + + + + + + + + + O + + + + +
+ + + + + + + + + + + + S + + + +
+ + + B R E C I B E + + + + E + + +
+ + + + E + + + + + + + + + B + + +
+ + + + + S + + + + + + + + + + +
+ + + + + + O + + + + + + + + + +
+ + + + + + + S + + + + + + + + +
+ + + + + + + + + + + + + + + + +
+ + + + + + + + + + + + + + + + +
```

(Over,Down,Direction)
ABRAZOS(6,7,NE)
BESOS(5,14,SE)
BESOS Y ABRAZOS(17,15,NW)
RECIBE(6,14,E)
UN ABRAZO(13,8,N)
UN FUERTE ABRAZO(14,7,W)

Juego 23 - Pg. 70

1. beso-kiss
2. abrazos-hugs
3. besos-kisses
4. recibe-receive
5. medicina-medicine
6. estás-you are
7. bien-well
8. cómo-how

24. La corrida de toros - Pg. 71

Across

3. el banderillero

Down

1. el picador
2. la muleta
3. el estoque
4. la capa
5. el toro

Juego 24 - Pg. 73

1. muleta
2. capa
3. estoque
4. picador
5. matador
6. banderillero
7. pase
8. toro

El fútbol 25 - Pg. 74

```
+ + + L + A O + + + + + + + E + + + +
+ + + O + S + R + + + + + L + + + + +
+ + + S + N + + I + + + + E A + + + + +
+ + + A + E + + + T + + N + P + + + +
+ + + F + F + + + L T + + A + + + +
+ + + I + E + E + + R E + + T + + + +
+ + + C + D + + L E + + + + A + + + +
+ + + I + A + + N E + + O I D E M L E +
+ + + O O L + A + + Q + + A + + + +
+ + + N + R D + + + + U + + + + + O +
+ + + A + O E + + + + + I + + + D + +
+ + + D R + + T + + + + + P + + I + + +
+ + + O + + + + N + + + + O T + + + +
+ + + S + + + + + A + + + + R + + E + +
+ + + + + + + + + L + + A + + L + + +
A T S I L O B T U F L E P + + B O + + +
+ + + + + + + + + + L D + A + G + + +
E L P O R T E R O + E + + L + + L + + +
+ + + + + + + + + + + Ó + E + E + + +
+ + + + + + + + + + + N + + + + + +
```

(Over,Down,Direction)
EL BALÓN(18,14,SW)
EL DELANTERO(15,19,NW)
EL ENTRENADOR(16,1,SW)
EL EQUIPO(8,6,SE)
EL FUTBOLISTA(12,16,W)
EL GOL(17,19,N)
EL MEDIO(19,8,W)
EL PARTIDO(11,18,NE)
EL PORTERO(1,18,E)
EL TIRO(12,6,NW)
LA DEFENSA(6,9,N)
LA PATADA(15,2,S)
LOS AFICIONADOS(4,1,S)

Juego 25 - Pg. 76

1. partido
2. equipo
3. portero
4. eestadio
5. gol
6. balón
7. defensa
8. patada
9. medio
10. tiro

ALSOP

110

26. La Navidad - Pg. 77

Across

2. la bola de nieve
6. los villancicos
8. los regalos
9. el árbol navideño
10. el hombre de nieve
11. la vela

Down

1. La Misa de Gallo
3. la iglesia
4. los nacimientos
5. La Nochebuena
6. la pastorela
7. Los Reyes Magos

Juego 26 - Pg. 79

1. mercado-market
2. posada-nine day celebration, inn
3. villancico-Christmas carol
4. la Misa de Gallo-Midnight Mass
5. árbol navideño-Christmas tree
6. nacimiento-Nativity scene
7. la Nochebuena-Christmas Eve
8. los Reyes Magos-the Three Kings
9. regalos-gifts
10. bola de nieve-snow ball

El Día de los Muertos 27 - Pg. 80

```
E + + + + + + + + + + L R + + + + S + L
H S + + + + + + + + A + + A + + A + + A
C + E + + + + + + S + + + + T D + + + S
O + + N + + + + V + + + + + N L + + + F
N + + O + + E + + + + + E + + A + + O
A + + + + E L + + + + + R + + + L + T
L + + + L A T + + + + F + + + + + E O
+ + + + S A + N + + O A D I M O C A L S
+ + + + + + S + A S + + + S + + + + + +
+ + + + + + + F A P + + A + + + + + + +
+ + + + + + + L L + S + + I + + + + + +
+ + + + + + + + O + O + L + + + + + + +
E L I N C I E N S O R + L I + + + + + +
+ + + + + + + + + + E + M + + + + + +
+ + + + + + + + + + + S A + + + N +
+ + + + + + + + + + + + F + + + A + +
+ + + + + + + + + + + + S + + P + +
S A R E V A L A C S A L + A + L + + + +
+ + + + + + + + + + + + + L E + + + + +
+ + + + + + + + + + + + + + + + + + + +
```

(Over, Down, Direction)
EL ALTAR(19,7,NW)
EL INCIENSO(1,13,E)
EL PAN(15,19,NE)
LA COMIDA(19,8,W)
LA NOCHE(1,7,N)
LAS CALAVERAS(12,18,W)
LAS FAMILIAS(14,19,N)
LAS FLORES(5,7,SE)
LAS FOTOS(20,1,S)
LAS OFRENDAS(8,11,NE)
LAS VELAS(12,1,SW)
LOS PANTEONES(13,13,NW)

Juego 27 - Pg. 82

1. vela-candle
2. ofrenda-offering
3. comida-food
4. calaveras-skulls
5. foto-photo
7. muertos-dead
8. flores-flowers
9. pan-bread
10. familia-family

28. La comida mexicana - Pg. 83
Across
3. los frijoles
4. las fresas
7. las enchiladas
9. las tortillas
10. el helado
13. la torta
14. los huevos
15. el flan
16. el bolillo
Down
1. la carne de res
2. el pollo
3. los chiles
4. los tacos al pastor
5. el melón
6. la lechuga
8. el arroz
11. los tomates
12. el queso

Juego 28 - Pg. 85
1. enchiladas-tortilla (dough)
   filled with chicken or meat
2. pollo-chicken
3. bolillo-roll
4. arroz-rice
5. fresas-strawberries
6. helado-ice cream
7. tortillas-corn or flour
8. maíz-corn
9. chiles-peppers
10. lechuga-lettuce

29. La comida - Pg. 86
española
Across
1. el flan
5. los calamares
6. la paella
7. los boquerones
8. el cordero
Down
1. el pan
2. el gazpacho
4. las patatas bravas

Juego 29 - Pg. 88
1. boquerones
2. merluza
3. pulpo
4. aceitunas
5. patatas bravas
6. flan
7. gazpacho
8. queso
9. cordero
10. paella
11. chorizo

La música latina 30 - Pg. 89

```
A + + + + Y + + + J + + + + + G + +
+ L + + N + + + U + + + + L + +
+ + E + + O A + S H A K I R A O + + +
+ + + J + H + R + + N + + R + + + +
+ + + + A T + + E + L + + I + + + +
+ + + + + N + + + V U + A + + + + +
S + + + + A D + + I E + + + + + + +
A + + + + C + R + + S R + + + + + +
N + + + + R + + O T G + Y + + + + + Z
T + + + + A + + E F U + + R + + + U +
A + + + + M + F + + E + L + R + + R + +
N + + + + + A + + + R R + A + E C + + +
A + + + + N + + + + R + N + I A J + + +
+ + + + + + + + + + A + + Á I N + + + +
+ + + + + + + + + + + + L N + D + + +
N I T R A M Y K C I R + E + + D + I + +
+ + + + + + + + + + + + C + + + E + A +
+ + + + + + + + + + + + + + + + Z + +
+ + + + + + + + + + + + + + + + + + +
+ + + + + + + + + + + + + + + + + + +
```

(Over,Down,Direction)
ALEJANDRO FERNÁNDEZ(1,1,SE)
CELIA CRUZ(12,17,NE)
GLORIA ESTEFAN(18,1,SW)
JERRY RIVERA(17,13,NW)
JUAN LUIS GUERRA(11,1,S)
LA INDIA(13,11,SE)
MARC ANTHONY(6,11,N)
RICKY MARTIN(11,16,W)
SANTANA(1,7,S)
SHAKIRA(9,3,E)

Juego 30 - Pg. 91

1. Ricky Martin
2. Shakira
3. Gloria Estefan
4. Jerry Rivera
5. Celia Cruz
6. Marc Anthony
7. Alejandro Fernández

31. Los animales - Pg. 92

Across

1. la cebra
4. el oso
6. el camello
7. el león
10. el gorila
11. el rinoceronte
12. el elefante

Down

2. el mono
3. el oso panda
5. la pantera
6. el tigre
8. la jirafa
9. la foca

Juego 31 - Pg. 94

1. elefante
2. tigre
3. caimán
4. camello
5. gorila
6. foca
7. flamenco
8. oso
9. leopardo
10. rinoceronte

Los pintores 32 - Pg. 95

```
+ + + + + + + + + + + + + F + + + + +
F + + + + + + + + + + + R + + + + + +
+ R + + + + + + + + + A Í + + + + + +
+ + I + + + + + + + + N L + + + + + +
+ + + D + + + + + + C + A + + + + + +
O + + + A + + + + I + + D + + + + + +
+ S + + + K + + S + + O R + + + + + +
+ + S + + + A C + + Y + O + + + + + +
+ + + A + + O H + + A + + D + + + + +
+ + + + C D + + L M + + + A + + + + +
+ + + + E I + + A O + + + V + + + + +
+ + + G + + P T + + + + L + + + + + +
+ + O + + + O O + + + + A + + + + + +
+ Y + + + N + + L + + + S + + + + + +
A + + + I + + + + B + + + + + + + + +
+ + + F + + + + + + A + + + + + + + +
+ + U + + + + + + + + P + + + + + + +
+ R + + + + D I E G O R I V E R A + + +
+ + + + + + + + + + + + + + + + + + +
+ + Z E U Q Z Á L E V O G E I D + + + +
```

(Over,Down,Direction)
DIEGO RIVERA(7,18,E)
DIEGO VELÁZQUEZ(16,20,W)
FRANCISCO DE GOYA(15,1,SW)
FRIDA KAHLO(1,2,SE)
PABLO PICASSO(12,17,NW)
RUFINO TAMAYO(2,18,NE)
SALVADOR DALí(14,14,N)

Juego 32 - Pg. 97

1. Pablo Picasso
2. Salvador Dalí
3. Francisco de Goya
4. Diego Rivera
5. Frida Kahlo
6. Rufino Tamayo
7. Diego Velázquez

Los escritores 33 - Pg. 98

```
+ G + + + + + + + + + + + + + S A + +
+ + U + + + + + + + + + + + E + C + +
+ + + S + + + + + + + + + T + + R + +
+ + + + T + + + + L + + + N + + O + +
+ + + + + A + + O + + + A + + + L + +
+ + + + + + V P + + + V + + + + A + +
+ + + + + + E O + + R + + + + + Í + +
+ + + + + D + + B E + + + + + C C + +
+ + + + E + + + C É + + + + + A R + +
+ + + V + + + E + + C + + + + R A + +
+ + E + + + D + + + + Q + + + L G + +
+ G + + + L + + + + + U + + O O + +
A + + + E + + + + + + E + + S C + +
+ + + U + + + + + + + + R + F I + +
+ + G + + + + + + + + + + + U R + +
+ I + + + + + + + + + + + + E E + +
M Z A P O I V A T C O + + + + N D + +
+ + + + + + + + + + + + + + + T E + +
S O R J U A N A D E L A C R U Z E F + +
+ + + + + + + + + + + + + + + S + + +
```

(Over,Down,Direction)
CARLOS FUENTES(17,8,S)
FEDERICO GARCÍA
LORCA(18,19,N)
GUSTAVO BÉCQUER(2,1,SE)
LOPE DE VEGA(10,4,SW)
MIGUEL DE
CERVANTES(1,17,NE)
OCTAVIO PAZ(11,17,W)
SOR JUANA DE LA CRUZ(1,19,E)

Juego 33 - Pg. 100

1. Miguel de Cervantes
2. Federico García Lorca
3. Lope de Vega
4. Gustavo Bécquer
5. Carlos Fuentes
6. Sor Juana de la Cruz
7. Octavio Paz

www.teachersdiscovery.com

ALSOP